Reconstruction in Religion

Reconstruction in Religion

A Symposium

Edited by

Alfred E. Kuenzli

Contributors

ERNEST E. BAYLES

HADLEY CANTRIL

BROCK CHISHOLM

RUDOLF DREIKURS

LAWRENCE K. FRANK

ERICH FROMM

JULIAN HUXLEY

SAMUEL JACOBS

Y. H. KRIKORIAN

ALFRED E. KUENZLI

FRANK W. NOTESTEIN

CARL R. ROGERS

THEODORE W. SCHULTZ

DONALD SNYGG

Beacon Press   Boston

Poetry, art, religion are precious things. They cannot be maintained by lingering in the past and futilely wishing to restore what the movement of events in science, industry, and politics has destroyed.

—JOHN DEWEY

Preface

It is widely agreed that this is a time of considerable social flux. Change, of course, creates conflict and out of conflict comes reconstruction. This reconstruction is not automatic but instead has to be nurtured and implemented. The new perspectives have to be articulated and the new ways have to be made functional in daily life.

Religion, the subject of this symposium, is one of the fields in which reconstruction has been taking place in recent years —a movement in the direction of what has been called "liberalism." The purpose of this symposium is to state some of the new views that have emerged and to point the way to further developments that need to take place.

The contributors are persons who are rooted in the behavioral sciences—psychology, psychiatry, sociology, anthropology, economics. They address themselves to mankind's most fundamental concerns—the search for faith, values, freedom and fulfillment within the natural and social world.

It is becoming increasingly clear that the traditional religions have not really answered, in any satisfactory sense, the major questions about human existence. Nor have they been of much real use when it comes to dealing with important social problems. One of the motivations underlying the symposium is the feeling that these basic concerns and problems are too important to be entrusted any longer to the meta-

physicians and priests. New sources of inspiration and guidance are appearing in our time and we need to see some of the
alternatives that are now available to us.

It is not necessary to document in detail, at this point,
the kind of dissatisfaction with traditional religions that is
being found in many parts of the world today. It shall suffice
to mention Hadley Cantril's *The Politics of Despair*, a very
provocative study of the protest voter in France and Italy.
That volume, based on field research by a team of social scientists, showed the widespread disillusionment with traditional
institutions and practices, particularly in the religious and economic spheres.

Professor Cantril concludes that more and more people
are questioning the adequacy of "many of the beliefs and
codes accepted by their forefathers and perhaps accepted by
themselves at an earlier age." They are beginning to sense
that existing power and status relationships may be standing
in the way of their further development and fruition. They
are searching for a new faith and for plans of action that
will help them to make some of their dreams come true.

The major premise underlying the symposium is that
the time has come for man to have *faith in himself*, in his
capacities for intelligent thought and action. Not only do
people *need* to have greater confidence in their capabilities
but also this is a time when they *can* have greater faith in
themselves because, increasingly, men are mastering the ways
of bringing about greater degrees of richness and satisfaction
for their lives.

As Theodore Schultz points out in these pages, the ancient notion that suffering is "God's will" is losing its force

in the modern world. "Men today will not be kept down in poverty because it is part of the symbolism of a caste or class or religion."

Frank Notestein suggests that people do not have to have whatever number of children "God sends," without regard to our capacity to provide them with opportunities for health, education and prosperity. But it will take time and effort to bring about the new outlook on human well-being that modern science has made possible.

A related premise underlying the planning of the symposium is that the most urgent task in the world today is to raise the living levels of the underprivileged peoples, who constitute almost 80 per cent of the world's population. The characteristic concern which liberals have for the welfare of their fellow men will just not let them rest comfortably in the presence of such widespread poverty and misery. Greater material gain is not, of course, an end in itself but is a requisite for moving on to a style of creative and satisfying living that will be worthy of human beings.

We are coming to see, however, that to bring about what John Dewey wanted, "the richest and fullest experience possible," is a very large and complicated order. One cannot get economic growth in the underdeveloped countries unless one limits population, but one cannot limit population until people are educated up to the point of being able to understand what it is all about. We are finding, furthermore, that if people are to move ahead it is necessary for them to have a world view that will be conducive to constructive action rather than to passive resignation.

A new spirit, a new climate of opinion, is in the making,

and it is this perspective which we have tried to capture between these covers. The kind of outlook that is developing
around us is aptly expressed in A. Eustace Haydon's phrase:
"What the gods have been expected to do, and have failed
to do through the ages, man must find the courage and intelligence to do for himself."

We are, then, living in "a world in ferment," an era of
accelerated social change. It is a time when people are ex-
amining the old ways and are looking for new ways. It is a
time when they *need* to have, and *can* have, greater confidence
in themselves. The new ingredient, the new source of hope,
is science and technology. The development, in our time, of
the physical, biological and social disciplines is providing mankind with new kinds of Promethean power. Just now, since
mid-century, has man been able to take his destiny into his
own hands and direct it for his own purposes—without re-
course to supernatural concepts.

The new faith will not be a shallow or naive optimism.
It will be fully aware of human shortcomings, as Julian Huxley
points out, and it will not expect more of people than is possible
at this stage in human emergence. It will not have its hopes
so high as to bring about continual disappointment. In Kurt
Lewin's terms, our "level of aspiration" will be both realistic
and challenging. Our strivings will be pitched to reasonable
next steps and will not, therefore, be utopian.

People need to make sense out of their lives, to find
authentic purposes and values and to help their children in
this quest. Religious liberals believe that man *can* understand
and develop, in a context of free inquiry, an increasingly
meaningful relationship to the natural and social world. It is
to be hoped that the materials presented in these pages will be

useful to the "fellowships of seekers"—to the various study groups that one finds within the Unitarian Universalist, Ethical Culture, Rationalist and Humanist movements.

By way of concrete suggestions, we have in mind that a study group might discuss these materials in six 2-hour sessions, taking one of the six sections of the book at each session. Since the first and last sections contain only one chapter each, that would leave more time at the beginning and end for introductory and concluding considerations.

Much more time, of course, could be fruitfully devoted to the issues raised in the various chapters. The contributors have listed suggestions for further reading at the conclusion of each chapter and these references could lead into intensive study on special topics.

An Overview

What is to be gained from reading and discussing the chapters in this symposium? What kinds of questions and issues are raised that are worthy of the reader's consideration? Perhaps a brief overview of the contents is in order as a conclusion to these prefatory remarks.

Part I anticipates the emergence of a new society in which men will live together in equality and brotherhood. It is argued that such a society, in contrast to the old authoritarian regimes, will need to have a democratic religion—one that will be based on human freedom, creativeness, courage and mutual aid. Questions are raised about our conventional moral codes, especially in the areas of family life and sexual behavior.

Part II is concerned with the problem of developing a rational, naturalistic perspective—a faith in oneself and others. These chapters examine the psychological conditions that bring faith into being and consider the function it has for the individual as he goes about the process of daily living. While —as perceptual research has shown—there can be no absolutes, we *can* develop reasonable guidelines for the conduct of personal and social life.

Part III focuses around the problem of values and related questions in the field of ethics. Understanding from recent research in the social sciences is brought to bear on questions in this area and the concept of "growth" or "fulfillment" is set forth as a basic moral principle.

Part IV is concerned with the nature, and further development, of human freedom. Barriers, both inside and outside the person, that stand in the way of the realization of freedom are examined and ways of overcoming these obstacles are discussed. It is suggested that it is important to free children's thinking from the "certainties" of previous generations and that a person's world view needs to be rooted in *his own* experiences and appreciations.

Part V makes a frontal attack on the problem of the poverty which still enslaves four-fifths of the world's population. An economist, a labor leader and a demographer challenge some of our assumptions in this field and show how we can bring about a more abundant life—both in the United States and among the less privileged peoples.

The theme in Part VI is that man's destiny is to be "the agent of evolution on this earth, realizing richer and ampler possibilities for the evolutionary process and providing greater fulfillment for more human beings." To pursue this

aim more effectively, it will be necessary to have a fully developed psychosocial science—a comprehensive discipline
which will help us to understand and nurture the potentialities
of the species.

In these chapters, then, the reader has an opportunity
to consider some of the basic problems involved in human
existence and emergence. As John Dewey has pointed out,
it is through the continuous appraisal of our beliefs, values
and practices that we move on to greater appreciations and
satisfactions. If the materials presented here prove to be useful
in terms of this kind of ongoing evaluative process, then the
symposium will have accomplished its purpose.

A. E. K.

Alton, Illinois

Contents

Preface   vii

I. Perspective
1. The Religion of the Future   RUDOLF DREIKURS   3

II. Faith
2. The Nature of Faith   HADLEY CANTRIL   23
3. Rational and Irrational Faith   ERICH FROMM   45
4. A Relativistic Religion   ERNEST E. BAYLES   59

III. Values
5. The Nature of Values   DONALD SNYGG   73
6. A Naturalistic Ethics   Y. H. KRIKORIAN   106
7. Social Science and Values   ALFRED E. KUENZLI   118

IV. Freedom
8. Freedom for the Personality   LAWRENCE K. FRANK   131
9. Tomorrow's Children   BROCK CHISHOLM   150
10. The Meaning of the Good Life   CARL R. ROGERS   173

V. Fulfillment
11. Human Wealth and Economic Growth
   THEODORE W. SCHULTZ   193
12. The Richer Rich and Poorer Poor   SAMUEL JACOBS   209
13. Poverty and Population   FRANK W. NOTESTEIN   224

VI. Epilogue

14. Man's Role in Nature   JULIAN HUXLEY   239

Contributors   250

Acknowledgments   252

Part I Perspective

1 The Religion of the Future

RUDOLF DREIKURS

We are living in a transitional period between two phases of mankind. Rapid and fundamental changes are taking place in our beliefs and practices as more and more people throughout the world throw off the yoke of autocracy and move in the direction of democracy.

Many people are beginning to wonder how "religion," in the traditional sense, will fare in the new societies. Will there be a new religion? If so, what will it be like? Is there any relationship between democracy and religion? Is any form of religion more appropriate for a democracy than another?

These are questions which merit careful consideration. To clarify the issues, we may well explore the definition and function of the terms "religion" and "democracy" and look into the historic development for guidance.

Religion and Democracy

Religion has often been defined as belief in supernatural forces. However, many persons reject this conception as being entirely too narrow. Actually, the term religion goes

3

back to Cicero and Lactantius. Cicero considered it in the sense of *religere*, meaning "to execute painstakingly by repeated efforts." Lactantius, on the other hand, attributed the term religion to *religare*, meaning "to bind together." Neither of the two interpretations of religious experiences and practices necessarily implies supernatural forces. One emphasizes the ritual of the recurring performance, and the other the subjective psychological experience of individual integration.

It is the function of religion to meet the needs of the group and of the individual. Religious activities are based on prevalent social and moral concepts; both change with each culture. Individual needs to be met by religion were always the same. Man is a social being, a *zoon politicon* (Aristotle), and, therefore, can function only within the group. His basic desire is to participate, to belong. Only by belonging to others can he function and find fulfillment.

Religious beliefs and practices integrate the individual firmly into his group, into society. The structure of society determines the forms of its religious activities. As John Dewey pointed out in his Terry lectures, there has been very little universality in the religious conceptions and forms of worship throughout the history of mankind.

In primitive society religion was mystic. Since primitive society had a strongly collective structure, primitive religion was predominantly collectivistic. Some authors believe that primitive religion originated in clan or tribe consciousness. It had no place for an individual deity since the individual was not conceived as such, but rather as part of the group.

During the period of civilization beginning six to eight thousand years ago, religious concepts changed in line with social changes. Tribal collectivism broke up and the individ-

ual emerged as an isolated particle in a heterogenous social
structure. Individual deities emerged. In contrast to the mystic nature of primitive religion, religion became deistic. Its
emphasis shifted from concern with natural forces to social
problems of behavior.

Religion became a highly individual experience. It re-
volved around personal sin and atonement of the individual,
especially with the spread of the Orphic Mysteries in Greece.
Individual communion gained particular ascendancy only in
the late Hellenistic period.

Individual gods behaved much as individuals did in society. As society moved toward unified autocracy, toward
monarchy, so did its gods. One God won over his rivals and
monotheism became the prevalent religious concept in the era
of contested rule by power. The divine autocracy reflected
the earthly rulers, monotheism the monarchy.

Let us now try to define "democracy." Many consider
it merely as a form of government, a political institution. But
it is much more than that; it is a specific structure of society
—characterized by a relationship of equality amongst all its
members. This distinguishes democracy from autocracy or
oligarchy (aristocracy) which was the predominant organization of society throughout our civilization.

In an autocracy, all relationships are those of superiors
and inferiors. This kind of relationship between individuals
and groups violates the basic laws of social living, the "iron-
clad logic of living together" (Alfred Adler) and, therefore,
does not permit cooperation and hence stable and harmonious
social interactions.

It was for this reason that the idea of democracy emerged
in antiquity as the only basis for social stability. The Greeks

coined the term democracy, rule by the people, in contrast to oligarchy, the rule of the few. It was the Greek Stoics who recognized and defined a fundamental human equality. Their ideal of human society has yet to be realized.

How did this emerging trend affect religious concepts? The Greek Stoics deprived Zeus of his "divine nature" and identified him with the universal and imminent "reason" or *Logos*. Their pantheistic religion had no place for divinities and the supernatural. The same Greek Stoics exerted their influence on Roman lawyers who, for the first time, based law on the recognition of human equality.

It was also the Stoic influence which inspired the early Christians in their belief in human equality. Those early Christians were the first group to put the idea of equality into practice. According to Gal. 3:28, all were equal before Christ —whether they be men or women, free or serf, Jews or Greeks. Christian congregations were for many centuries conspicuous for granting women and serfs equal status with free men.

However, this obvious trend toward democracy at the end of the ancient culture could not bear fruit. One of the factors responsible for its collapse was that the ancient culture was based on a slave society. With the exception of the small group of Christians, slaves were denied the status of equality and dignity. And these very slaves destroyed the Roman Empire and its culture. The only remnant through the ensuing Dark Ages was Christianity with its concept of human equality and dignity.

Some adjustment to the regression of social and political conditions was mandatory. The idea of equality of man gave way to the Augustinian doctrine which established medieval orthodoxy. Worldly inequality became part of the divine scheme of things and a consequence of a fall willed by God. The emerging concept of original sin and predestination deprived man of his intrinsic dignity.

A similar development occurred in Asia. As a reflection of growing democratic trends, Buddhism discarded the metaphysics of Brahmanism and, in its original form, was atheistic. But, like Christianity, Buddhism "regressed" from a simple formula for living to supernatural concepts. This religion started at the end of the ancient cycle of culture, with its democratic development, and survived through the Middle Ages—adjusting to the autocratic social and political climate of that period.

The Rise of Rationalism

The correlations between political evolution and religious concepts should be obvious at this point. Subsequent developments in human history make it clear that a revolt against the supernatural coincided with democratic emergence. As the democratic trend gradually overcame the autocratic tradition, rationalism struggled against supernaturalism, scientific research against revelation.

The term "rationalism" first appeared in the religious sphere during the Renaissance together with the rediscovery of historical democratic concepts. Renaissance humanists were inspired by a revulsion from medieval reliance on authority and the subordination of reason to it; they tried to vindicate the autonomy of reason over the authority of books and institutions.

English religious philosophy of the sixteenth and seventeenth centuries called "Rationalists" those who considered reason the highest authority—not only in science but also in matters relating to religion and society. In the Netherlands in that time it was customary to distinguish between "rational" and "nonrational" theologians.

It was especially in England, the land of democracy, and through Herbert of Cherbury (around 1600) that religious rationalism was founded and clearly formulated. Reason was considered to possess in itself the capacity for all truth, including the religious and moral. The dogma of original sin or corruption of reason through the fall of man was unconditionally rejected. Spinoza followed Uriel Acosta and Daniel de Prado in his opposition to supernaturalism.

This development was entirely within the religious sphere. Out of this concern came modern science. Rationalism inspired Copernicus, Galileo, Kepler and especially Descartes. Scientific progress—as well as art, music and philosophy—developed within the sphere of religion since at that time religion was the whole way of life, encompassing all human cultural activities.

With the development of democracy, mankind entered a new phase of social organization. Human relationships, which were characterized by dominance and submission during the authoritarian era, began to change to a basis of equality. God as a symbol of supreme power, protecting the rights of those who on earth maintained their superiority over others, became a controversial figure. The individual—realizing his own value and dignity—deposed not only kings, emperors and tyrants but also the divine aristocracy. Millions turned away from their belief in a supreme being.

This development brings us to the question: Will this

third—the democratic—phase of human culture be without any specific religion, or will it evolve its own religion in line with its new social perspectives? There can be no doubt that each of the two previous cultural phases of mankind—primitive society and aristocratic civilization—had its own specific form of religion, each completely different from the other. Any religious expression of the democratic cultural era will have to be equally idiomatic. But will there be a new religion? And if so, what form will it take?

Aspects of the New Religion

The "spiritual needs" of mankind do not require supernatural concepts. They merely call for an orientation which can lift individuals out of the daily tribulations and provide perspectives *sub specie aeternitatis*—under the aspects of eternity. A new society will need its own religion because society needs orientation—crystallization of its concepts and perspectives, its morals and values.

To be sure, this new and universal religion does not exist as yet. Nobody can say what it will be like. But certain features of the future democratic religion are becoming clear. Let us consider several aspects of this emerging perspective.

1. *The new religion will probably be humanistic.* It will be concerned with man and not with God. The concept of a personal God, of a power outside our natural experience, does not fit a scientifically oriented way of life among individuals who are becoming aware of their independence and self-determination, of their strength and force within themselves.

A new picture of the world and of man in it, as Julian

Huxley has pointed out, is emerging as a result of the newest scientific discoveries. Self-determination and inner freedom are becoming recognized as an intrinsic part of all existence, including inorganic matter. Man is discovering that all this strength and power which inspire his awe when he beholds a thunderstorm, a raging stream or waterfall, a snowcapped mountain in all its majesty—that this power of life not only surrounds and threatens him from without but is *within him* and at his own personal disposal.

Each individual human being, with all his tremendous abilities and power, deserves a comparable awe and admiration because of his intricate biological functioning as well as his complex mental and emotional capacities. Man is a creator. He does not merely react to whatever may impress him, he acts and moves actively. The powers around him cannot be divided into supreme or less supreme powers. Within himself and about him he is confronted with life and has to find a way of meeting it satisfactorily. That is the essence of a humanistic orientation in regard to the universe.

2. *Religious truth will be scientific truth.* But this truth will be of a fundamentally different nature than previous generations and cultures could ever have visualized. There is no longer an absolute truth. Absolutes exist only in an autocracy where a power has established itself to dictate what is truth. Truth is reality, but man can perceive reality only in a limited way. Therefore he can find only *approximations* to truth, not the absolute—not the *Ding an sich* of Kant. Relativity replaces absolutes.

But within this restricted field of the knowable, our scientific research, and not revelation, can provide information. And what we can know is sufficient to permit adequate

living so that we do not have to concern ourselves with what
we cannot know.

Only in a democratic era will the exploration of truth and
scientific research be free. It never has been so in the past. Religious authorities or socially dominant groups restricted what
could be known. Many Galilei are still sacrificed because their
discoveries do not suit those who have the power to control. The democratic religion will oppose such powers as the
Christian religion opposes the devil. The interest of society is
preserved by its religious concepts; the democratic society will
develop religious concepts which guarantee the democratic
process for the benefit of all.

3. *Religious prescriptions will serve new morals.* What
the moral concepts of a democracy will be, nobody can say.
New moral values are emerging with the present democratic
evolution and many time-honored traditional moral concepts
are crumbling. A new society will require new moral regula-
tions, different from a past cultural period. We are still en-
meshed in the tradition of an autocratic past; therefore we
cannot visualize clearly the perspectives which eventually
will emerge. Living in a period of transition between two
great cultural eras, we merely witness the inadequacy and
open bankruptcy of values which were kept in high esteem
in the past and are becoming futile or even dangerous at the
present.

Changes in Family Ideals

Our intimate contacts with the problems of modern family life, be it in marital counseling or child guidance, reveal the

confusing and threatening condition in which we are living. Signposts which have governed man throughout past centuries have become invalid, and many persons are uninformed about new directions for proper behavior.

A man who is overambitious, a hard worker and devoted to his job, may be highly successful in his business or profession, a respected member of his community, an excellent provider, taking care of all the needs of his family—so he thinks. But if one can look behind the facade of respectability and success, one becomes aware of what he is actually doing to his family. His wife has no chance for self-expression. She is deprived of any useful contribution to the community if this is done on a professional level and involves income; in other words, she is not permitted to take on a job where her training and ability might be utilized.

And if you look at his son, you see his dilemma and tragic predicament. He is impressed with the significance of superior masculinity; he wants to be a "real man" like his father. But at the same time he sees no chance of ever amounting to anything. He is sure, by comparison with his father, that he is not really a man. The high demands of his father often prevent him from achieving anything; so he may switch to the useless side of life to gain importance and significance —by defiance, misbehavior and similar asocial and often destructive methods. All the highly valued qualities of superior masculinity become a hazard in the close family relationship within a democratic setting.

The very same fate befalls a woman who lives up to the feminine ideals of a "good woman." So many women of our time try desperately to be good, to do right. Their endeavor is understandable through their desire to become equal to a man—and perhaps even to surpass him—in an era of democratic equality where they no longer want to be relegated to the role of the second sex. And they succeed in becoming good; they study hard, apply themselves, become orderly, concerned with social standards and conformity. And they become such good wives and mothers that neither husband nor children have a chance to do anything right.

If any one quality could be pointed out as being most responsible for the difficulties which a mother has with her children, it is her effort to be so good. Consequently, she overprotects her children, does what the child could do for himself, makes demands which he cannot meet, tries to prevent dangers which do not exist—and the child has no experience of his own strength, no chance to take responsibility. The mother is certainly a "good" woman—but her goodness becomes a destructive force.

These two examples of the futility and even malignancy of traditional masculine and feminine ideals indicate the need for a careful scrutiny of all heretofore accepted moral values and standards for behavior. Ambition, righteousness, conformity, perfectionism and similar qualities—stimulated and highly praised in an autocracy—are no longer sufficient to bring good results in a world of free men, in a relationship between equals. It is no longer sufficient to be good and successful. Fulfillment of one's own life, living in peace and harmony, requires different qualities, or at least modification of established codes. Instead of ambition we may need enthusiasm; instead of righteousness, friendliness and understanding. Mere conformity will not stimulate improvement; courage to be imperfect will prove to be healthier and more beneficial than perfectionism has been.

One area that may require the most obvious change is the one to which common language most frequently refers when we speak about morals, that is, the sexual code. Most religions have concerned themselves greatly with regulating sexual behavior. Characteristic for our traditional European-American culture were prescriptions for sexual behavior which were generally ignored. Monogamy has been established by religious and legal demands; but it was never practiced—at least not by men. The rules of chastity were imposed only on women and the social consensus permitted extramarital relationships for men. The main principle in proper male sexual behavior in the past was *secrecy*. Everything was condoned as long as it was kept secret from women. Men could do as they pleased sexually, and only women were restrained.

This is no longer true for our present-day society. Men and women have reached a status of social equality which never existed before in the whole history of mankind. Consequently, special privileges of men are no longer accepted and transgressions on the part of women are not as much frowned upon, compared with the standards of the past. Monogamy is probably more frequent today than it has been throughout past centuries; but so is greater sexual freedom for women. Some may think that we have no moral code because the old code is obviously no longer enforced. But there can be no doubt that a new code is developing.

Again it is difficult to predict what the sexual code of a democratic society will be. Different cultures have different sexual prescriptions. The democratic society cannot accept double standards for men and women. The new code will take into consideration both the elements of freedom and of responsibility. It will be neither rigidly repressive nor licentious. Such a morality will be in line with realistic practices and not a false front, a pretense which nobody sincerely accepts. This fact, plus the absence of a tendency to keep one part of society—one sex—in ignorance so that it can be better exploited by the other, will probably change essentially the social conventions—removing the air of secrecy which surrounded sexual behavior in the past. This tendency is already well evident; the proponents of progress clash with the adherents of the past in the question of sex education. It is the same clash which is evident between new forms of religion and the old ones.

While we can be certain that existing social and moral values will give way to new concepts, the question arises as to how this will be done. It is society itself, mankind as such, which moves toward change in its groping for more adequate forms of living—more adequate for fulfillment of the individual and for greater harmony between all. That is how progress has been achieved, how political systems have evolved, how morals and conventions arose. We may say that all these developments take place through changes in general practice and through the emergence of leaders who express the needs of the group and get their support from the members of the group whose ideals they represent and confirm.

Moral values are established by practice; they express group interaction and group consensus. But the maintenance and codification of newly established values and principles requires leadership which can verbalize and clearly express what people feel, think and want. This was the function of religion throughout the ages. The members and the leaders of a new religion have the obligation to formulate a new philosophy and to implement it with practical recommendations for daily living.

From Fear to Courage

New symbols will be needed. This is perhaps the greatest deficiency of modern humanism; it has failed to provide effective and generally acceptable symbols. Symbols are sign posts which evoke specific emotional attitudes. They are short-cuts in persuasion and motivation. They evoke almost automatic responses from those who accept them. They do not require explanations because they are understood. They are necessary for group cohesion and group movement. The new religion will need them because without them it cannot be a religion or a social force.

We can only speculate as to what kind of symbols will emerge. One seems rather probable, in distinction to the basic symbol of orthodox religions: the concept of sin. Sin is the embodiment of all that is bad, all that should be avoided. But this concept of sin requires an authority who declares what sin is.

Sin is an atavism in a democratic social organization. People act badly not because of their sinful make-up but because they are misguided. They are not bad, but discouraged. There will be no room for sin in a democratic religion. Whoever is wrong or "bad" needs help, *understanding and treatment*, not condemnation and punishment. Karl Menninger, among others, has recently shown that our present system of penology is "an utter failure" and proposes that criminals should be rehabilitated through a therapeutic program.

Many contemporary social convulsions are the result of the decreasing power of authorities in a world where all are becoming equals. Our parents and teachers experience their defeat on the part of the whole generation of children who are becoming our equals and require a different treatment from that which traditional education and principles entail. Even our imprisoned criminals revolt if they are not treated with dignity and respect. The new methods which prove effective and which are based on an understanding of both individual psychodynamics and group dynamics do not resort to punitive retaliation. And yet they are more effective—or better said, they alone are effective in our democratic atmosphere.

Today the symbol of the bad, or of "sin," is *fear*. Fear was an integral part of orthodox religion; it was used to keep the inferior in line. The threat of punishment on this earth and in the hereafter was designed to create fear as a deterrent to transgression. Fear today is recognized as the greatest obstacle to fulfillment and function, to self-respect and self-realization.

Far from preventing transgressions and misdeeds, fear actually promotes them. It increases rather than diminishes the probability of danger. One does not have to be afraid of automobiles in order to cross a street safely. But a person who is afraid of being hit by a car is more likely to incur an accident. Fear is evil; it deprives us of strength, poise, clear evaluation of the situation and the determination to solve problems.

In contrast, *courage* seems to be one of the requirements of free men. The new religion will need a symbol which evokes courage, belief in one's own strength and ability. Our new concept of the universe necessitates courage. Modern man needs courage to face uncertainties, since certainties are assured only in an autocracy. Modern man needs courage because he recognizes his own spontaneity and creativeness— and it requires courage to be spontaneous. Spontaneity is a prerequisite to self-fulfillment. It is opposed to submission, to conformity for conformity's sake.

Courage is impaired by doubts about our status and worth. The assumption of our deficiency restricts our willingness and ability to cooperate and to be concerned with the welfare of others. Only a courageous person who knows his strength and has faith in himself can have faith in others; only such a person can accept the give-and-take of social living. A sense of responsibility cannot be instilled in free men by fear but only through their feeling of belonging, their awareness of their interrelatedness, the sureness of their own place and their worth as persons.

The Ritual of Mutual Aid

The religious ritual will consist of mutual aid. The spiritual and moral support which we all need in the discouraging tribulations in our daily lives can only come from the group where we are truly one another's brother. We need each other's help in our efforts to be as good as we want to be and to be as effective as we can be. We need each other to remind us of our ideals and to give us the persistence to pursue them. We need each other to stimulate our devotion to the common good, to stir up our willingness, to feel with each other, to live with each other, to belong to each other.

The religion of the future will be capable of combining the collective experience of primitive society with the individual self-realization of civilization. It will be able to use reason and present-day knowledge to stir up our emotions, to bring out the best in each of us, to evoke attitudes of cooperation and courage and to give us the resilience to resist the temptation of our own selfish interests and prejudices. It can and will provide the tools to realize the brotherhood of man.

Such a religion cannot be authoritarian, only humanistic. Its faith is in man, not in God. Its truth must be found through human investigation, not through revelation. Its moral perspectives will be those of free men; its symbols will free man of his fears. And finally, its ritual will consist of mutual help so that we each can be the self-determined and self-respecting master of our fate, creator of the world around us and benefactor of this tremendous force of life around and in us.

Bibliography

Adler, A. *Social Interest: A Challenge to Mankind*. London: Faber & Faber, 1938.

Black, A. D. "Can Humanism Meet Man's Spiritual Needs?" *Humanist*, 1959, 19, 195-206.

Buehrer, E. T. "Retracing the Liberal Tradition," *Humanist*, 1960, 20, 133-142.

Dewey, J. *A Common Faith*. New Haven: Yale University Press, 1934.

Dreikurs, R. *The Challenge of Parenthood*. New York: Duell, Sloan & Pearce, 1948.

————. *The Challenge of Marriage*. New York: Duell, Sloan & Pearce, 1946.

————. *Character Education and Spiritual Values in an Anxious Age*. Boston: Beacon Press, 1952.

————. "Raising Children in a Democracy," *Humanist*, 1958, 18, 77-83.

————. "A Humanistic View of Sex," *Humanist*, 1959, 19, 84-92.

Foote, A. "New Dimensions in Liberal Religion," *Unity*, 1960, 145, 136-143.

Huxley, J. *Religion Without Revelation*. Rev. ed. New York: New American Library, 1957.

Leuba, J. H. *The Reformation of the Churches*. Boston: Beacon Press, 1950.

Menninger, K. "Verdict Guilty—Now What?" *Harper's*, 1959, 219:1311, 60-64.

Rafton, H. R. "What Can We Believe?" *Humanist*, 1953, 13, 118-124.

Smith, H. W. *Man and His Gods*. Boston: Little, Brown, 1953.

Part II Faith

2   The Nature of Faith

HADLEY CANTRIL

The experience of "faith" is one of the most real, yet one of the most ineffable, characteristics of human living. Without this capacity, human nature would be far different than it is. And so would all of man's social and political organizations.

For the process we call "faith" plays the crucial role of holding our values together and of integrating our purposes. Without this unifying factor, living would be a much more hit-and-miss affair; it would be much less directed. And it would be empty of many of the value overtones that we lump together as those that make living worthwhile.

Faith has turned notorious sinners into saints. By means of faith, ordinary men have performed extraordinary miracles. When faith was aroused, dejected masses have been transformed into revolutionary crusaders. Faith, said the prophet, can move mountains.

Nearly all of us in our own lives can testify to the "reality" of some faith—perhaps a faith we have experienced in something or someone, a faith that kept us plugging along when the going was unusually tough, a faith that altered our lives to some degree when we felt hopelessly bogged down.

23

Or perhaps we have experienced the feeling of emptiness and isolation when we have "lost" our faith or had it shaken at the very roots.

In spite of the importance of faith in the process of living, contemporary psychology has rarely met the problem of "faith" head-on. In fact, psychological mention of the subject is even hard to find in the literature.

We shall examine here systematically the psychological conditions under which faith comes into being and the function it has for the individual as he goes about the process of living. Faith will be considered as a crucial aspect, as a reality, characterizing some of man's experience, except for which many of the transactions of life would not be what they are.

What does the word "faith" refer to?

In order to answer this question, we must examine some of the conditions and circumstances without which people would not have the experience of faith—or would not even know they were lacking in faith.

The Awareness of Faith

We are only occasionally aware of faith or of the need for faith. Most people most of the time are not at all aware of any aspect of faith as they go about their daily life routines. Usually we are too preoccupied with the present and with a "present" which we seem able to cope with in ordinary ways, without requiring the support that faith can provide.

We become aware of faith or of the need for faith only under certain conditions. And we would have no need for faith at all if the world were static with everything neatly determined and predictable. For in such an ordered world our lives would be characterized by certainties and repeatabilities. And they would, of course, be deadly monotonous, even worse than the life of a prison inmate confined for the rest of his days.

But as everyone knows, we are not living in a static world. Change and flow are the rule. And change and flow are accompanied by the unforeseen and the unexpected. Because the future is not entirely determined and predictable, experience for most of us frequently carries at least mild overtones of concern which we can label "anxiety," "excitement," "curiosity" or "doubt," depending upon the circumstances.

Living therefore inevitably creates constant frustrations. The frequency and severity of these frustrations of course depend upon the fortunes of our personal life histories, including our ability to meet frustrations. For millions of underprivileged people there may be little else than frustration.

But whoever we are, there is never complete certainty about the next moment, the next day or the next year. We always have to do some guessing. All of us have to weigh some probabilities in a world which is an open system. In *The King and I*, the bewildered King of Siam sings: "There are times I almost think I am not sure of what I absolutely know. Very often find confusion in conclusion I concluded long ago."

The same idea is illustrated in an incident which Carl Sandburg describes in his autobiography, *Always the Young Strangers*:

I have always enjoyed riding up front in a smoking car, in a seat back of the "deadheads," the railroaders going back to the home base. Their talk about each other runs free . . . Once I saw a young fireman in overalls take a seat and slouch down easy and comfortable. After a while a brakeman in blue uniform came along and planted himself alongside the fireman. They didn't say anything. The train ran along. The two of them didn't even look at each other. Then the brakeman, looking straight ahead, was saying, "Well, what do you know today?" and kept looking straight ahead till suddenly he turned and stared the fireman in the face, adding, "For sure." I thought it was a keen and intelligent question. "What do you know today—*for sure?*" I remember the answer. It came slow and honest. The fireman made it plain what he knew that day for sure: "Not a damn thing!"

Most of us are generally not as aware of our uncertainties as the lovable king or the wise fireman. For when something happens that goes counter to our assumptions, we are at least surprised; the unexpected event negates some aspect of our reality world on which we have counted for constancy.

The nature of the reaction we have to the unexpected situation will depend on the nature of the occasion. Perhaps we will experience disappointment or resentment, perhaps suspicion or mistrust, perhaps shock or grief, perhaps worry or despair. Or our experience may be one of laughter or joy, buoyancy or hope, gratitude or admiration.

Situations that provoke faith are always situations where *value, worth and importance* are involved. And situations that provoke faith are always situations where *choice and responsibility* come in, where there are possibilities that mistakes may be made, mistakes that may be ours. Situations that we handle with reflexes and habits involve a sense of "surety," not a sense of "faith," except in the unusual cases.

In the many varied circumstances of living, we can usefully differentiate three different conditions that give rise to faith or the need for faith.

1. We become aware of faith or the need for faith when we *lack confidence in our ability to cope satisfactorily with our present situation.* We are anxious because we are won-

dering if we will make it. The workman on a new job, the student in an examination, the scientist carrying out an experiment, the mother raising her child, the surgeon performing a difficult operation, the public servant assuming a more responsible office, the farmer trying a new crop, are a few of the infinite variety of human conditions that may arouse in the participant an awareness of faith.

2. We become aware of faith or the need for faith when we feel we are simply *unable to accept or accede to some events or conditions that have occurred in the past*. We are unable to live at peace with ourselves in the present because we are haunted by the past. We blame ourselves, castigate ourselves. Or we resent what others appear to us to have done. Or we are upset by some condition we feel was brought about by impersonal forces.

The consequences of this situation take various forms. We may refuse to recognize either our own limitations or the influences that have been part of a cause of past disappointments or failures. We may keep trying to push out of our consciousness certain memories or responsibilities that we feel we handled badly. We may keep harboring a grudge against people or circumstances.

3. We become aware of faith or the need for faith when we are *apprehensive about the foreseeable future*, even though we accept the past and are confident enough about the present. In this condition we are filled with doubts and misgivings when we look ahead. Since we have no clear prehension of steps we might take to bring about the experiencing of certain goals we have in mind, we are apprehensive. How are we going to earn a better living? How will we get ahead? How will we maintain or improve our health? How can we give our

children the opportunities we want them to have? How can we get more security in our lives? How can we obtain or give more affection and love? How can we make sure there will be no more depressions or wars?

In any of these three conditions or a combination of them, we cannot enjoy a sense of complete well-being. We may come to doubt seriously the reliability of *the reality world* we have built up—the only world we know. Our experience may become tinged with a sense of disappointment, a sense of inadequacy. We may become unusually depressed. We may feel a lack of appreciation from others. We may feel a gnawing guilt, painful agony, miserable inferiority, flaming jealousy or complete despair.

But far from being calamities, such unpleasant or painful experiences are the essential preliminary processes that catalyze faith or develop greater faith. *Faith is born of frustration; faith is kindled and nourished by difficulties.*

It is only through frustrations that we can achieve more workable assumptions. And it is only by experiencing *obstacles to be overcome* that we can develop faith. If there is a rare individual who has never felt frustration or has never faced an obstacle to overcome, then his faith, if he has any, is purely intellectual and untried. Like a bubble, it will burst when pricked.

The Capacity for Faith

One of the basic requirements of human beings is the need to preserve the sense of the worthwhileness of living. To do this, we create a subjective reality world—a system of interpretations—that functions with passable adequacy in an ever-changing cosmos.

Since our experience is so much a matter of probability, of the bets we are constantly making in a changing world as to the characteristics of things, of people, of events, we *must* do something to put order and repeatability into the world in which we carry on our living. We are more comfortable if we think we can predict with a fair degree of accuracy the chain of events that will occur if we undertake a certain action. We crave certainty rather than doubt. We want enough form and pattern in our thoughts and feelings to give direction to flow.

So we create *constancies* concerning things, people and events. We attribute certain consistent characteristics to them so that we shall be provided with enough interpretation to guess with fair accuracy what the significances and meanings are of the variety of signals that reach our sense organs, without having to make fresh guesses at every turn.

All of these significances that we build up about objects, people, events, symbols or ideas fuse and orchestrate together to give us our own unique reality world. Everything that has significance for us takes on its significance from our own personal behavioral center—in terms of *our own* purposes and *our own* actions. These significances become more or less common depending upon the experiences and purposes we share with other people.

But in addition to these personal significances which we take into account as we participate in one occasion after another, we also utilize in our living the significances conveyed by the *abstractions* man has created through the ages. Man has devised these abstractions in his perpetual attempt to bring order into disorder, to explain to himself various types of phenomena or to find universal principles and guides for more ordered living, no matter what the unique purposes or circumstances of any one individual may be.

Among such abstractions are our scientific formulations, our maps, our legal, ethical, political and religious systems. They can be recalled or referred to at will. They can be experienced by anyone at any time since they are repeatable, fixed, spelled out and formulated. They can become universal.

And there are other abstractions that man uses—abstractions represented by symbolic forms in art, in music and in religion. These are more difficult to conceptualize or to put into words.

All of these abstractions are by their very nature fixed and static. Hence they can never become true substitutes for the personal meanings and significances assigned to events. For the abstraction cannot take into account the unique contingency any unique individual is likely to meet in life any more than a scientific formulation concerning the behavior of atoms can predict the behavior of a single atom.

Nevertheless, these abstracted conceptions of reality can and do play a most indispensable role in helping us through our periods of frustration and doubt if and when our personal reality systems prove strained or inadequate. When the *tangibles* of our personal reality worlds break down, we can turn to the *intangibles*. We can recall those abstractions that have been created by others and that have proved useful to others. We can apply them to the particular problem we face. We can make ourselves aware of creeds, beliefs, parables, maxims, aesthetic representations of moods. We can recall as a symbol for ourselves the courageous or appropriate behavior of others who have faced similar crises.

If we can put the abstraction to work for us, *if* we can use it as a basis for *our* choice and action in the undetermined situation *we* face here and now, then we can transform the abstraction into a personal reality. But the abstraction becomes real *only* if it becomes functional in *our own* behavior. For when it becomes functional, we can experience what the abstraction refers to. Then we may get the exciting or profound sense of a fleeting identity with something more universal—a sense of identity with abstract "truth," "love," "mankind," "nature" or "God."

Men thus have the capacity to sense the experience of the imminent becoming transcendent, of the particular becoming universal, as some abstraction—not bounded by intervals of time or units of space—becomes relevant and operational in the concreteness of the here and now of a person's own behavioral center. It is this capacity of man to *recall* and to utilize relevant abstractions that makes it possible for him to have an abiding faith, a faith which transcends time and space. It is this capacity to *create* and to utilize relevant abstractions that makes it possible for men to share their faith with people in all ages and places and to *communicate* their faith to others.

What Faith Involves

"Faith," said the prophet, "is the substance of things hoped for; the evidence of things not seen." Less eloquently we can say that, psychologically, faith is a bet on, a commitment to or a value sense of *the worthwhileness of a personal reality system* composed of constancies that serve as guides to purposive action.

Our understanding of what faith "is" can be more complete if we see what faith "involves," what some of the factors are except for which faith would not be experienced. All of the aspects of faith noted here are, of course, interdependent.

1. *Faith is intensely personal.* It must be yours. Only *you* can experience your faith; only *you* can test it.

Faith must always have some referent; it must always be "about" or "in" something or someone. Just as a lover cannot be "in love with love" until he is in love with someone, so faith cannot be brought into awareness unless and until some transaction of living poses a problem that puts faith or the need for faith into operation.

This obvious point must be stressed to emphasize again the profound difference between *experiencing* what faith refers to and simply recalling some abstraction intellectually or giving lip service to it.

2. *Faith involves some participation in the flow of events, some action, some doing.* "Faith without works is dead." It is only in the quality of experience sensed from the consequences of action that faith is created, restored, confirmed or expanded.

While the achievement of an intended goal is important, if the accomplishment of the goal is itself taken as the only criterion of faith, then that faith must prove temporary. For if we cannot foresee further potential value satisfactions ahead, then what faith we have will be empty.

3. *For faith to be enduring, a goal must serve as a step to other goals.* "A goal is a signpost," said John Dewey at the age of ninety. It is in the *process* of participation and doing that one is aware of a sustaining faith. And in the sequence of goals that give some direction to living, there is potentially

the satisfaction of *personal growth* and "enrichment," as one discovers and tests new or more inclusive assumptions and value standards—with the overtone that faith is being confirmed or enlarged.

4. *Faith requires a sense of assurance that means can be followed or devised to bring about the experiencing of intended goals.* Assurance, in the sense of absolute certainty, is almost never possible. But if faith is to "exist" and become functional, an individual must be able to feel that he has a workable, common-sense chance of being able to influence events that involve him. He must feel a reasonable degree of confidence in the effectiveness of the methods available to him to reach his objective.

For if we have a sense of the potential goals that may be ahead for us but at the same time have no conceivable or only the most remote prospect of realizing those goals, then faith will be difficult to sustain. This can often be seen in a person who is in virtual slavery; in the overworked, poorly paid laborer who sees no freedom from his bondage; in the industrial automaton who seeks only escape; or in the individual who finds himself in a spiritual vacuum because his faith in some creed or set of beliefs has been destroyed by events or by an education that has given him no viable substitute.

5. *Faith requires that the sense of self-constancy be maintained.* If the constancy of "self" is upset, it becomes difficult to assess change and accommodate to it. We lose the compass that keeps us going in a direction. We don't know what significances to take into account. "We" are lost.

When we say that self-constancy must be maintained, we do not imply that there can be no growth or development. On the contrary, self-development is itself an aspect of self-constancy. But development must flow from form if it is to be recognized. Without such flow from form there is no standard for comparison, no sure sense of continuity.

This means that our sense of "self" and our faith in that "self" must constantly be reaffirmed through *our participation with others*. For our feeling of "self," and our own self-constancy and self-significance, are determined to a large extent by our significance to other people and the way they behave toward us.

We must, of course, rid ourselves of any notion of an abstract "self" (or ego) that can somehow be isolated, pointed to, analyzed or experienced apart from any social context. The idea of an abstract self seems to be what the prophets were inveighing against when they preached that we "find ourselves" by "losing ourselves." They seem to be insisting that we not make the mistake of abstracting a nonexistent "self" out of a life-setting which alone gives it meaning.

6. *Faith is made real only when hope is confirmed.* As St. Paul observed, faith involves the hope of experiencing potentially attainable goals. Hope is confirmed through experiencing the consequences of action. And if action does not sooner or later bring about the sense that hopes are being realized, then faith will be abandoned.

Without the aspect of hope, faith could never work the miracles it does. And without the aspect of hope, faith could not involve as it often does the overtone of transcendent wonder as we experience the "full" significance of present, past and probable future events.

Hope, like frustration, is a necessary condition for personal development and for the emergence of new value-satisfactions. In a most real sense, the realization of hope through faith *is* emergence.

7. *Faith requires a sense of the worthwhileness of living and of the value of life itself.* A feeling that living is worthwhile usually involves some sense of appreciation from others. For if most human beings are to live at all, they must live among their fellow men. This means that the satisfaction we can experience from the consequences of our own actions is in a large measure a satisfaction derived from the feeling that *other people appreciate our actions,* or will appreciate them. This bolsters the sense of the worthwhileness of living, of the value of you yourself and of your responsibility to others.

The highest expression of this appreciation is, of course, what we call "love"—where your own well-being depends on furthering another person's well-being and, reciprocally, where another person's satisfaction is dependent upon experiencing the consequences of action that provide you maximum satisfaction and well-being. The most profound love is the most universal love, the love of "all mankind," of "all living things." For a Jesus, a St. Francis or a Gandhi, universal love is a cornerstone of the faith they tried to demonstrate.

The sense of the worthwhileness of living is dependent upon the sense of worthwhileness of the reality world which the person has built up, with its constancies that serve as reliable guides to purposive action. A most crucial aspect of faith, if it is to be an aspect of living that has reality, is *the sense of identification which the individual has with the values that faith represents and pulls together.* If this identification is passive and provides only a one-way street leading from abstract values to the personal life, then faith is likely to be only an escape. It will involve no great sense of personal responsibility and will require no active integration of the individual's various purposes. Nor will it demand any particular consistency between knowledge and belief.

Such a faith may become a blind idolatry, with worship of gods or images which may suddenly prove inadequate in some personal crisis. But if, on the other hand, faith plays an active role in living, then it takes on more of the nature of *an engagement or a commitment*, a dedication to a set of principles or beliefs which it becomes the person's responsibility to try to apply and make real in the ongoing, changing situations that constitute living.

Keeping the Faith

The great majority of people in the world are "born into" a faith represented by some codified, institutionalized religion or some political unit. They learn very early from their elders some pattern of values. It is *imposed* upon them. They may get more satisfaction from it than they are often willing to acknowledge. They see that it "works" in their own lives.

In order to perpetuate these formalized constancies and provide the possibility that they will acquire common and standardized significances and meanings, all institutionalized religions and political systems have devised their own pattern of ritual and ceremony. Participation in such rituals enables the believer to associate himself through his own action with the abstraction the ritual symbolizes—whether it is telling his beads, saluting a flag, or bowing his head.

While many people, to be sure, take part in such ceremonies with tongue in cheek or without really sensing any
involvement or significance in what they are doing, still for
the vast majority there is a sense of being tuned in with more
universal standards. In the process, the individual's faith in his
own standards—the standards he lives by—is confirmed. His
faith is self-validated by repeating the constancies of a ritual.

From the beginning of time man has apparently sought
some ultimate, universal constancy that would serve as a reposi-
tory, protector and fountainhead of all his most personal and
most cherished values and aspirations. In all ages, men have
apparently searched for some sort of God and have, in their
search, brought forth all manner of deities according to their
needs. The concept of "God" makes it easy for people to get
hold of their value constancies, hang on to them, and keep
them fixed.

In accounting for this search for God and in understanding the function that God has for the believer, we should recall some of the conditions that give rise to the need for faith:
frustrations, disappointments, agonies, unfilled hopes. These
conditions are also necessary to bring about the search for
God.

Man's amazing capacity to help create an environment
within which he can carry out his purposes and mitigate some
of his problems enables him to obtain reassurance that his God
is working with him. Hence God *can* become part of human
experience if he is sensed as a *process*. On the other hand, if
God is a mere intellectual abstraction, he can never play a role
in living, can never be demonstrated or experienced. "The
Kingdom of God is among you," said Jesus.

Acquiring a Personal Faith

As man learns more and more about nature and the universe of which he is a part, he questions more and more the validity of any faith which involves supernatural explanation or forces.

But at the same time, the sense of being on his own without the aid of some outside friendly agent also increases man's feeling of helplessness and his sense of urgency for something to believe in. If man cannot create a new faith for himself from his knowledge alone, still he at least doesn't want knowledge to stand in the way of a faith. For he continues to seek a set of beliefs—a set of beliefs consistent with what he knows.

The ardent Roman Catholic or Buddhist can identify himself with beliefs that function for him and are confirmed by his daily rituals. The Communist militant faithfully follows the discipline of the party. But the individual who has no rigidly set institutionalized creed to adhere to must in a sense *create his own faith* and sustain this faith through his own transactions of living.

Yet man's increasing knowledge of the world around him and of himself makes his craving for certainties and absolutes harder to satisfy and to justify. The quest seems to be that of finding a "cause" that represents value aspirations which men can share in a scientific age, aspirations which men can dedicate themselves to and try to experience in their own living by effective participation with others.

Circumstances seem to be forcing people to the realization that their relations with others are the crucial problem for their own well-being and for their survival. *The question of faith seems to be becoming more and more a question of how to acquire faith in other people and how to instill in other people a faith in us.* It is the ancient problem of acquiring and demonstrating compassion, charity and love.

When we look for constancies in other people and for correspondence between what we think they are and how they turn out to be when we participate with them, a variety of complications is introduced. For other people have their own purposes, often difficult for us to understand. Their purposes will change as conditions change and as their behavior progresses from one goal to another. *Their* purposes and behavior are affected by *our* purposes and behavior, just as *ours* are affected by *theirs*. When we deal with people, constancies and repeatabilities are not easy to find.

As noted earlier, in an attempt to increase the meanings and significances people have in common, societies have developed all manner of customs, mores, conventions, laws and other codes of behavior. And as people sense more and more their interdependence upon each other, both as individuals and as citizens of nations, old forms are revised and new common links are devised in the attempt to keep purposes emerging and compatible with required behavior.

All of these social forms presumably serve the function of improving the degree of correspondence between what is in our awareness and what is *potentially* in the social environment to be aware of. And the reason for attempting to increase this correspondence is, of course, to provide purposeful action of a more predictable direction and with a greater chance to repeat itself in satisfying ways—with more certain value-constancies.

The process is, and always will be, a never-ending one. For correspondence where people are involved can never be perfect. Increased correspondence in our social perceptions of each other will inevitably be accompanied by increased satisfactions, which themselves will point to new potential satisfactions.

In this ceaseless process, the individual searching for faith gets support for his value-standards from others who seem to share them—his family, his friends and the various groups he identifies himself with. As long as they help him carry out his purposes by their actions, help him maintain and develop his own self-constancy, he will find them fortifying his faith and deserving of it. But, to repeat, it is only in time of *personal crisis* and emergency when this faith in people is manifested and filters into awareness. At other times it is part of the relatively normal, "neutral" world; it is *potentially* with us and we may take it into account in our behavior even though we are not aware of it.

A person will be able to become more aware of faith and to gain faith when he is able to see the *potential* values in living which he has not sensed before *and* when he feels there is a good chance that he will be able to participate effectively in bringing about these potential value-satisfactions in his own experience.

But if his doubts and frustrations are continually unresolved through action, he is likely to find himself in a *psychotic* condition where he either lacks surety concerning the present, where he refuses to accept the past or where he is unduly apprehensive about the future. In each case, faith and hope are abandoned and can only be re-established by painstaking relearning and reconditioning.

Such reconditioning will require above all else a therapy which simplifies goals so that their accomplishment will be assured through the individual's own action, thereby rebuilding his confidence in himself. Once self-confidence is regained on a simple level, goals can gradually be raised. What holds for a single individual also holds for members of a group or culture.

The problem of gaining faith is closely related to the ancient problem of "insight." The recognition of our own adequacies and inadequacies in terms of the goals we have set for accomplishment can help restore faith in those cases where the self-assessment has been inaccurate, where persons consequently suffer from a constant sense of inadequacy because they are aiming at the wrong things or are looking in the wrong place for satisfaction to appear. Frequently the counsel of a wise friend or a skilled therapist will aid in clarifying goals and simplifying means.

The process of self-examination can bring into awareness purposes we had heretofore not recognized as guiding our actions. It can also release latent abilities which we may have only vaguely sensed and insufficiently nurtured.

The Need for Value Inquiry

The inquiry we must undertake to gain faith is the sort which we can label "value inquiry" as contrasted to logical or rational inquiry. It involves "mulling things over," "meditation," "communion" or "prayer." Its purpose is to allow us to sensitize ourselves to our feelings, to reflect on the priority and weight we should assign to different value standards and to get *a sense of orchestration* into various aspirations and responsibilities we feel are right for us.

For value inquiry to occur unhampered, we must insulate ourselves from here and now pressures. Christ went to the top of the mountain and Gandhi had his day of silence. The faithful Hindu sets aside a certain period each day for uninterrupted meditation. Only by getting away from immediate obligations and routines can our conscious and unconscious processes, together with our feelings, flow unhampered in surveying the widest possible range of cues to take into account in making our value judgments. It takes time. It requires leisure and is doubtless the reason why so many of the great original thoughts that have come into the world have occurred to their creator when he was relaxed while walking, sitting under an apple tree or taking his bath.

In the West we have badly neglected to educate ourselves to the processes involved in such value inquiry. We seldom even pose the question of how to make such value inquiry more worthwhile by increasing our sensitivity to the potential value-satisfaction inherent in the many occasions of living. This is essentially the true function of religious literature, of prayer and meditation.

Only through learning and practicing value inquiry can we get a sense of the full significances potentially available to us in our behavior. Only then can we guess the probable long-range consequences that our actions will have on us and on the purposes of others. Only then can we see how to improve the quality of our satisfactions by improving the quality of our purposes and the quality of our actions. Only then can we begin to simplify our lives, learning that if we become sensitive to value cues we can then become aware of how even our smallest daily actions hold a possibility of transcending the immediate moment and taking on more universal value significance.

Thus, by building up our value standards, sensing their confirmation in action, and discovering revisions that will make them more encompassing, we can develop a faith of sufficient power to weather the inevitable frustrations and deprivations we will encounter. Faith enables us to feel that, come what may, life is full of unpredictable and satisfying promises which can be brought into fruition if we will participate purposefully and responsibly in the flow of events.

And faith makes it possible for us to see that death itself is the beginning of the "everlasting life" which we have as the result of the effects of our behavior on others and on still others yet to come in the long line of humanity ahead.

Bibliography

Bentley, A. F. *Inquiry into Inquiries*. Boston: Beacon Press, 1954.

Buber, M. *I and Thou*. New York: Scribner, 1937.

Cantril, H. *The "Why" of Man's Experience*. New York: Macmillan, 1950.

———. *The Politics of Despair*. New York: Basic Books, 1958.

———, & Bumstead, C. H. *Reflections on the Human Venture*. New York: New York University Press, 1960.

Dewey, J. *A Common Faith*. New Haven: Yale University Press, 1934.

———, & Bentley, A. F. *Knowing and the Known*. Boston: Beacon Press, 1949.

Haydon, A. E. *Biography of the Gods*. New York: Macmillan, 1941.

Kilpatrick, F. P. *Explorations in Transactional Psychology*. New York: New York University Press, 1961.

Macmurray, J. *The Self As Agent.* London: Faber & Faber, 1957.

Otto, M. *Science and the Moral Life.* New York: New American Library, 1949.

Shahani, R. "The Great Humanists of India," *Humanist*, 1960, 20, 36-41.

Taylor, E. *Richer by Asia.* Boston: Houghton Mifflin, 1947.

3 Rational and Irrational Faith

ERICH FROMM

Faith is not one of the concepts that fits into the intellectual climate of the present-day world. One usually associates faith with God and with religious doctrines, in contradistinction to rational and scientific thinking. The latter is assumed to refer to the realm of facts, distinguished from a realm transcending facts where scientific thinking has no place and only faith rules. To many, this division is untenable. If faith cannot be reconciled with rational thinking, it has to be eliminated as an anachronistic remnant of earlier stages of culture and replaced by science—by facts and theories which are intelligible and can be validated.

The modern attitude toward faith was reached after a long struggle against the authority of the church and its claim to control any kind of thinking. Thus skepticism with regard to faith is bound up with the very advance of reason. This constructive side of modern skepticism, however, has a reverse side which has been neglected.

Insight into the character structure of modern man and the contemporary social scene leads to the realization that the current widespread lack of faith no longer has the progressive aspect it had generations ago. Then the fight against faith

was a fight for emancipation from spiritual shackles and irrational belief. Today the lack of faith is the expression of profound confusion and despair.

Can man live without faith? Must not the nursling have
"faith in his mother's breast"? Must we all not have faith in
our fellow men, in those whom we love and in ourselves? Can
we live without faith in the validity of norms for our life? Indeed, without faith man becomes sterile, hopeless and afraid to
the very core of his being.

Was, then, the fight against faith idle and were the
achievements of reason ineffectual? Must we return to religion
or resign ourselves to live without faith? Is faith necessarily a
matter of belief in God or in religious doctrines? Is it linked
so closely with religion as to have to share its destiny? Is faith
by necessity in contrast to, or divorced from, rational thinking?

I shall attempt to show that these questions can be answered by considering faith to be a basic *attitude* of a person, a
character trait which pervades all his experiences, which enables a man to face reality without illusions and yet to live by
his faith. It is difficult to think of faith not primarily as faith
in something, but of faith as an inner attitude the specific object of which is of secondary importance. It may be helpful
to remember that the term "faith" as it is used in the Old Tes-
tament—"Emunah"—means "firmness" and thereby denotes
a certain quality of human experience, a character trait, rather
than the content of a belief in something.

The Problem of Doubt

For understanding the problem of faith, it may be helpful to approach it by first discussing the problem of doubt.
Doubt, too, is usually understood as doubt or perplexity concerning this or that assumption, idea or person, but it can also
be described as an *attitude* which permeates one's personality,
so that the particular object on which one fastens one's doubt
is of but secondary importance. In order to understand the
phenomenon of doubt, one must differentiate between *rational*
and *irrational* doubt. I shall presently make this same discrimination with regard to the phenomenon of faith.

Irrational doubt is not the intellectual reaction to an
improper or plainly mistaken assumption, but rather the doubt
which colors a person's life emotionally and intellectually. To
him, there is no experience in any sphere of life which has the
quality of certainty; everything is doubtful, nothing is certain.

The most extreme form of irrational doubt is the neurotic compulsion to doubt. The person beset by it is compulsively driven to doubt everything he thinks about or to be per-
plexed by everything he does. The doubt often refers to the
most important questions and decisions in life. It often in-
trudes upon trifling decisions, such as which suit to wear and
whether or not to go to a party. Regardless of the objects of
the doubt, whether they are trifling or important, irrational
doubt is agonizing and exhausting.

The psychoanalytic inquiry into the mechanism of compulsive doubts shows that they are the rationalized expression
of unconscious emotional conflicts, resulting from a lack of

integration of the total personality and from an intense feeling
of powerlessness and helplessness. Only by recognizing the
roots of the doubt can one overcome the paralysis of will
which springs from the inner experience of powerlessness.
When such insight has not been attained, substitute solutions
are found which, while unsatisfactory, at least do away with
the tormenting manifest doubts. One of these substitutes is
compulsive activity in which the person is able to find temporary relief. Another is the acceptance of some "faith" in which
a person submerges, as it were, himself and his doubts.

The typical form of contemporary doubt, however, is
not the active one described above but rather an attitude of
indifference in which *everything is possible, nothing is certain.* An increasing number of people are feeling confused
about everything—work, politics, morals and, what is worse,
they believe this very confusion to be a normal state of mind.
They feel isolated, bewildered and powerless; they do not experience life in terms of their own thoughts, emotions and
sense perceptions but, instead, in terms of the experiences they
are supposed to have. Although in these automatized persons
doubt has disappeared, indifference and emptiness have taken
its place.

In contrast to irrational doubt, *rational doubt* questions
those assumptions which depend, for their validity, on belief
in an authority and not on one's own experience. This kind of
doubt has an important function in personality development.
The child at first accepts all ideas on the unquestioned authority of his parents. In the process of emancipating himself from
their authority, in developing his own self, he becomes critical. In the process of growing up, the child starts to doubt the

legends he previously accepted without question, and the increase of his critical capacities is directly proportionate to his becoming independent of parental authority and to his becoming an adult.

Historically, rational doubt is one of the mainsprings of modern thought. Through it, modern philosophy and modern science received their most fruitful impulses. Here, too, as in personal development, the rise of rational doubt was linked with the growing emancipation from authority—that of the church and the state.

Faith and Authority

In regard to *faith*, I wish to make the same differentiation which was made with regard to doubt: the differentiation between rational and irrational faith. By irrational faith I understand the belief in a person, idea or symbol which does not result from one's own experience of thought or feeling, but which is based on one's emotional submission to irrational authority.

Before we go on, the connection between submission and intellectual and emotional processes must be explored further. There is ample evidence that a person who has given up his inner dependence and submitted to an authority tends to substitute the authority's experience for his own. The most impressive illustration is to be found in the hypnotic situation where a person surrenders to the authority of another and, in the state of hypnotic sleep, is ready to think and feel what the hypnotist "makes him" think and feel. Even after he has awakened from the hypnotic sleep he will follow suggestions given by the hypnotist, though thinking that he is following his own judgment and initiative.

While the hypnotic situation is the most conclusive experiment in demonstrating the interrelation between submission to an authority and thought processes, there are many relatively commonplace situations revealing the same mechanism. The reaction of people to a leader equipped with a strong power of suggestion is an example of a semi-hypnotic situation. Here, too, the unqualified acceptance of his ideas is not rooted in the listeners' conviction based upon their own thinking or their critical appraisal of the ideas presented to them, but instead in their emotional submission to the speaker.

People in this situation have the illusion that they agree, that they rationally approve of the ideas the speaker suggested. They feel that they accept him because they agree with his ideas. In reality the sequence is the opposite: they accept his ideas because they have submitted to his authority in a semi-hypnotic fashion.

For irrational faith, the sentence "*Credo quia absurdum est*"—"I believe *because* it is absurd"—has full psychological validity. If somebody makes a statement which is rationally sound, he does what—in principle—everybody else can do. If, however, he dares to make a statement which is rationally absurd, he shows by this very fact that he has transcended the faculty of common sense and thus has a magic power which puts him above the average person.

Among the abundance of historical examples of irrational faith, it would seem that the Biblical report of the liberation of the Jews from the Egyptian yoke is one of the most remarkable comments on the problem of faith. In the whole report, the Jews are described as people who—though suffering from their enslavement—are afraid to rebel and unwilling to lose the security they have as slaves. They understand only the language of power, which they are afraid of but submit to. Moses, objecting to God's command that he announce himself as God's representative, says that the Jews will not believe in a god whose name they do not even know. God, although not wanting to assume a name, does so in order to satisfy the Jews' quest for certainty.

Moses insists that even a name is not sufficient surety to make the Jews have faith in God. So God makes a further concession. He teaches Moses to perform miracles "in order that they may have faith that God appeared to you, the God of their fathers, the God of Abraham, Isaac and Jacob." The profound irony of this sentence is unmistakable. If the Jews had the kind of faith which God wished them to have, it would have been rooted in their own experience or the history of their nation. But they had become slaves; their faith was that of slaves and rooted in submission to power which proves its strength by its magic. They could be impressed only by another magic, not different from but only stronger than the one the Egyptians used.

The most drastic contemporary phenomenon of irrational faith is the faith in dictatorial leaders. Its defenders attempt to prove the genuineness of this faith by pointing to the fact that millions are ready to die for it. If faith is to be defined in terms of blind allegiance to a person or cause and measured by the readiness to give one's life for it, then indeed the faith of the Prophets in justice and love, and their opponents' faith in power, is basically the same phenomenon—different only in its object. Then the faith of the defenders of freedom and that of their oppressors is only different inasmuch as it is a faith in different ideas.

Faith and Productiveness

Irrational faith is a fanatic conviction in somebody or something, rooted in submission to a personal or impersonal irrational authority. Rational faith, in contrast, is a firm conviction based on productive intellectual and emotional activity. In rational thinking, in which faith is supposed to have no place, rational faith is an important component. How does the scientist, for instance, arrive at a new discovery? Does he start with making experiment after experiment, gathering fact after fact without having a vision of what he expects to find? Rarely has any important discovery in any field been made in this way. Nor have people arrived at important conclusions when they were merely chasing a fantasy.

The process of creative thinking in any field of human endeavor often starts with what may be called a "rational vision," itself a result of considerable previous study, reflective thinking and observation. When the scientist succeeds in gathering enough data or in working out a mathematical formulation, or both, to make his original vision highly plausible he may be said to have arrived at a tentative hypothesis. A careful analysis of the hypothesis in order to discern its implications and the amassing of data which support it lead to a more adequate hypothesis and eventually perhaps to its inclusion in a wide-ranging theory.

The history of science is replete with instances of faith in reason and vision of truth. Copernicus, Kepler, Galileo and

Newton were all imbued with an unshakable faith in reason. For this, Bruno was burned at the stake and Spinoza suffered excommunication. At every step from the conception of a rational vision to the formulation of a theory, *faith* is necessary —faith in the vision as a rationally valid aim to pursue, faith in the hypothesis as a likely and plausible proposition and faith in the final theory, at least until a general consensus about its validity has been reached. This faith is rooted in one's own experience, in the confidence in one's power of thought, observation and judgment. While irrational faith is the acceptance of something as true only *because* an authority or the majority say so, rational faith is rooted in an independent conviction based upon one's own productive observing and thinking.

Thought and judgment are not the only realm of experience in which rational faith is manifested. In the sphere of human relations, faith is an indispensable quality of any significant friendship or love. "Having faith" in another person means to be certain of the reliability and unchangeability of his fundamental attitudes, of the core of his personality. By this I do not mean that a person may not change his opinions but that his basic motivations remain the same—for instance, his capacity or respect for human dignity is part of his self, not subject to change.

In the same sense we have faith in ourselves. We are aware of the existence of a self, of a core in our personality which is unchangeable and which persists throughout our life in spite of varying circumstances and regardless of certain changes in opinions and feelings. It is this core which is the reality behind the word "I" and on which our conviction of our own identity is based. Unless we have faith in the persistence of our self, our feeling of identity is threatened and we become dependent on other people whose approval then becomes the basis for our feeling of identity with ourselves. Only the person who has faith in himself is able to be faithful to others because only he can be sure that he will be the same at a future time as he is today and, therefore, will be able to feel and act as he now expects to. Faith in oneself is a condition of our ability to promise something, and since—as Nietzsche pointed out—man can be defined by his capacity to promise, that is one of the conditions of human existence.

Another meaning of having faith in a person refers to the faith we have in the potentialities of others, of ourselves and of mankind. The most rudimentary form in which this faith exists is the faith which the mother has toward her newborn baby —that it will live, grow, walk and talk. However, the development of the child in this respect occurs with such regularity that the expectation of it does not seem to require faith. It is different with those potentialities which can fail to develop —the child's potentialities to love, to be happy, to use his reason and more specific potentialities like artistic gifts. They are the seeds which grow and become manifest if the proper conditions for their development are given, and they can be stifled if these conditions are absent.

One of the most important factors is that the significant persons in a child's life have faith in these potentialities. The presence of this faith makes the difference between education and manipulation. Education is identical with helping the child realize his potentialities. The opposite of education is manipulation, which is based on the absence of faith in the growth of potentialities and on the conviction that a child will be right only if the adults put into him what is desirable and cut off what seems to be undesirable. There is no need to have faith in the robot since there is no life in it.

The faith in others has its culmination in faith in mankind. In the Western world this faith was expressed in religious terms in the Judaeo-Christian religion, and in secular language it has found its strongest expression in the progressive political and social ideas of the last one hundred and fifty years. Like the faith in the child, it is based on the idea that the potentialities of man are such that—given the proper conditions—he will be capable of building a social order governed by principles of equality, justice and love. Man has not yet achieved the building of such an order and, therefore, the conviction that he *can* requires faith. But like all rational faith this, too, is not wishful thinking but is based upon the evidence of the past achievements of the human race and on the inner experience of each individual—on his own experience of reason and love.

While irrational faith is rooted in the submission to a power which is felt to be overwhelmingly strong, omniscient and omnipotent—in the abdication of one's own power and strength—rational faith is based upon the opposite experience. We have this faith in a thought because it is a result of our own observation and thinking. We have faith in the potentialities of others, in our own and in mankind's because—and only to the degree to which—we have experienced the growth of our own potentialities, the reality of growth in ourselves, the strength of our own power of reason and of love. *The basis of rational faith is productiveness.* To live by our faith means to live productively and to have the only certainty which exists —the certainty growing from productive activity and from the experience that each one of us is the active subject on whom these activities are predicated.

Faith and Power

It follows that the belief in power (in the sense of domination) and the use of power are the reverse of faith. To believe in power that exists is identical with disbelief in the growth of potentialities which are as yet unrealized. It is a prediction of the future based solely on the manifest present; but it turns out to be a grave miscalculation, profoundly irrational in its oversight of human potentialities and human growth. There is no rational faith in power. There is submission to it or, on the part of those who have it, the wish to keep it. While to many power seems to be the most real of all things, the history of man has proved it to be the most unstable of all human achievements. Because of the fact that faith and power are mutually exclusive, all religions and political systems which originally are built on rational faith become corrupt and eventually lose what strength they have if they rely on power or even ally themselves with it.

One misconception concerning faith must be briefly mentioned here. It is often assumed that faith is a state in which one passively waits for the realization of one's hope. While this is characteristic of irrational faith, it follows from our discussion that it is never true for rational faith. Inasmuch as rational faith is rooted in the experience of one's own productiveness, it cannot be passive but must be the expression of genuine inner activity. An old Jewish legend expresses this thought vividly. When Moses threw the wand into the Red

Sea, the sea—quite contrary to the expected miracle—did not divide itself to leave a dry passage for the Jews. Not until the first man had jumped into the sea did the promised miracle happen and the waves recede.

At the outset of this discussion I differentiated between faith as an attitude—as a character trait—and faith as the belief in certain ideas or people. So far we have dealt only with faith in the former sense and the question poses itself now whether there is any connection between faith as a character trait and the objects in which one has faith. It follows from our analysis of rational as against irrational faith that such a connection exists. Since rational faith is based upon our own productive experience, nothing can be its object which transcends human experience.

Furthermore, it follows that we cannot speak of rational faith when a person believes in the ideas of love, reason and justice, not as a result of his own experience, but only because he has been taught such belief. Religious faith can be of either kind. Some sects that did not share in the power of the church and some mystical currents in religion that emphasized man's own power to love—his likeness to God—have been the main forces in preserving and cultivating the attitude of rational faith in religious symbolism.

What holds true of religion holds true for faith in its secular form—particularly in political and social ideas. The ideas of freedom and democracy deteriorate into nothing but irrational faith once they are not based upon the productive experience of each individual but are, instead, presented to him by parties or states which force him to believe in these ideas.

Man cannot live without faith. The crucial question for our own generation and the next ones is whether this faith will be an irrational faith in leaders, machines, success, or the rational faith in man based on the experience of our own productive activity.

Bibliography

Dewey, J. *Human Nature and Conduct*. New York: Modern Library, 1930.

———. *A Common Faith*. New Haven: Yale University Press, 1934.

Fromm, E. *Escape from Freedom*. New York: Rinehart, 1941.

———. *Man for Himself*. New York: Rinehart, 1947.

———. *Psychoanalysis and Religion*. New Haven: Yale University Press, 1950.

———. *The Sane Society*. New York: Rinehart, 1955.

———. *The Art of Loving*. New York: Harper, 1956.

——— et al. *Zen Buddhism and Psychoanalysis*. New York: Harper, 1960.

May, R. *Man's Search for Himself*. New York: Norton, 1953.

Moustakas, C. E. (ed.). *The Self: Explorations in Personal Growth*. New York: Harper, 1956.

Wertheimer, M. *Productive Thinking*. New York: Harper, 1945. Enlarged edition, 1959.

4 A Relativistic Religion

ERNEST E. BAYLES

This article might well have been titled "The Religion of John Dewey," for the religion of Dewey is a logical outgrowth of his overall philosophy—the philosophy of relativism. But I wish to deal with the question of religion from a broadly relativistic standpoint rather than confine myself to the matter as Dewey himself expressed it; hence the more generalized title.

The philosophy of relativism (more commonly called pragmatism, instrumentalism or experimentalism) may conveniently be said to take its start in recognition of the proposition that an object or event can neither be perceived nor conceived as a thing-in-itself, that it can be humanly dealt with only as a figure against a background and viewed by an observer from a given vantage point and in light of the ideas or insights which he possesses. In other words, in light of experiential and experimental knowledge available today, human observations cannot be taken as thoroughly passive, mirror-like reflections of the light waves and other sensory stimuli which come to an observer, as John Locke and Isaac Newton took them to be. On the contrary, human perception never gets beyond the status of *human interpretation* of what comes to the perceiver in the form of light rays, sound waves, etc. Perception as well as conception is a cooperative affair, dependent both upon the view*er* and the view*ee*.

This principle means that nothing can be taken by human beings as existing in and unto itself alone, as self-dependent or autonomous, as separate or absolved from all else, *as absolute.* This is not an explicit denial that some or many things in the universe may be that way. It is merely the assumption that human beings have no warrant for taking them to be that way—for assuming absolutes—and that it therefore behooves human beings to plan and execute their lives on the basis of refusal to assume absolutes.

The Nature of Absolutes

A philosophic absolute is an entity which is completely and totally not subject to, nor affected by, anything other than itself. Hence, philosophic absolutes have to be taken as utterly beyond human contrivance of any kind. For example, if a moral code such as the Ten Commandments is so considered, then it must be taken as sacrosanct, to be altered by human convictions in no way, shape or form. The sixth Commandment, "Thou shalt not kill," is then an absolute right; any shading or modification whatever represents wrong, utter and absolute. In absoluteness there are no degrees. Perfect is perfect.

Perhaps someone wishes to say that no one nowadays thinks of the Ten Commandments in this manner. But that is exactly the point of relativization. Any exception whatever represents human intervention and destroys any claim to absoluteness. Yet one can hardly read with care the account in Exodus of the deliverance of the Ten Commandments and fail to catch the thorough intention that they be considered God-given absolutes. The whole pattern of thought underlying the principle of cosmic rectitude and of truth which can be ascertained by man only through revelation from on high is an absolutistic one. Right is right and true is true, whether man likes it or not. One cannot go half way with absolutes; it is either all or none. That is what relativistic thinkers realize and, frankly recognizing that it is humanly impossible to be genuinely absolutistic on any proposition, they set out consciously to erect a program for living which is overtly and unapologetically relativistic.

Such a purpose means adoption of the proposition that all human plans are based on what the planners *take* the world to be, not on what it "really is." And this applies, whether we are concerned with the realm of truths or the realm of values. Justification both for what is taken as true and for what is taken as right is to be found in human experience, not in some "higher deliverance." To insist that something is true or is right because God made it so is, perhaps, merely an excuse to justify one's unwillingness to subject one's beliefs and convictions to open and rational consideration. To put it bluntly, a relativist is disinclined to use God as a shield behind which to hide because he is either unwilling or unable to fight his own battles. Any and all propositions are taken to be true or false, right or wrong, because human experience has shown them to be so—not because God made them so.

Believing versus Knowing

It should be noted, however, that a relativist is required
by the logic of his philosophical premises *neither to assert nor
to deny* that God created the universe, that God created the
truths of the universe, that God created the orderliness of nature, that God determined what is right and what is wrong.
For the very nature of our assumptions regarding God places
Him beyond the realm of human knowing, and a relativist con-
siders it unjustifiable to say that he knows when indeed he
does not and cannot. A relativist may believe, or disbelieve, in
God. That is a strictly personal matter. For it is quite my right
as a person to believe or disbelieve in something even though
I may have for it no rational or valid justification. Difficulty
arises only when I go further and say, "I know." Believing is
one thing; knowing is quite another.

Relativistic philosophy makes belief distinctly personal.
It may be well, or poorly, grounded—whichever the individual wishes it to be. On the other hand, knowing is taken as
something distinctly beyond individual whim. The one and
only sanction for saying, "I know," is *anticipatory accuracy*—
the accuracy in anticipating or predicting future events which
the proposition in question enables a user to achieve.

In noting that relativistic premises logically require
neither assertion nor denial of the existence of God, we bring
out the point that the relativistic position is neither theistic nor
atheistic. For theism represents adherence to the proposition
that God exists, whereas atheism represents adherence to the
proposition that God does not exist. Nor, contrary to state-

ments frequently made, does the relativistic position represent agnosticism. For agnosticism is basically theistic, adherence to the proposition that God and absolute truth do indeed exist but, being infinite, are quite beyond the reach of finite minds.

Man's Self-Dependence

But what, if not personal belief, do relativistic premises logically require? Seemingly, it is a working agreement to plan actions and live lives on the basis of the *assumption*—not the assertion—of self-dependence. Even though harboring a conviction of the existence of God, a relativist may not with consistency use such faith as a workaday principle. Such faith may be a luxury; the luxury is not denied. But, do not the hard facts of life seem to indicate that man's own intelligence and wisdom comprise the best means which mankind now possesses for determining the ends, ways and means of planning and achieving his destiny? Even Oliver Cromwell seems to have been of this persuasion when, in an address to troops before crossing a river to attack an enemy, he advised, "Put your trust in God; but mind to keep your powder dry!"

If it appears that we cannot really depend on God to extricate us from our difficulties, we had perhaps better make the assumption that we have to depend upon ourselves, and set up a program for living in accordance therewith. In this way we secure the advantage of whatever we can do for ourselves and, in addition, of whatever help God may be able or willing to give. For, if God possesses the attributes of love and forgiveness and of more than common human decency which are attributed to Him, He can hardly be else than gratified with us for doing what we can for ourselves. Was it not *Poor Richard's Almanac* which assured us that "God helps them who help themselves"?

What we have been saying seems to add up to a position which can be characterized neither as theistic nor atheistic nor even agnostic, but as *nontheistic*. As to assertions regarding God, there is none to be made. But as to assumptions, we have to assume self-dependence. We have to deal with a world which is not of our making except only as we participate directly in such making. But we have to deal with it on moral-ethical bases and with truths which we can hardly take as other than homemade. Can we, with sound justification, either credit or blame God for them? Perhaps it is something like an author's statement in the preface of a book wherein he generously acknowledges help from various sources but assures his readers that he must take the rap for what the book contains.

A Nontheistic Religion

It would seem that we are now ready to consider the question, "Is a nontheistic religion possible and, if so, what might be some of its salient points?" With reference to this question, we can let Dewey do much of the ball-carrying because it is to this question that he has addressed himself in *A Common Faith*.

First, in attempting to reach a working definition of *religion* or *religious*, he indulges in several pages of speculation as to what articles or article of faith might be found common to all religions or religionists. And, as might be expected, he finds no specific article of creed or belief regarding which there is consensus or agreement. As to the immaculate conception or even the divinity of Jesus Christ, there is great divergence even among Christian faiths. As to the vehicle for God's revelation, divergence is multifarious. As to the nature of God Himself, there seem to be almost as many different beliefs as there are believers.

The upshot of Dewey's thinking may be roughly expressed by saying that, if there is anything common to the aims, aspirations or convictions of mankind which may be called religious, it must be the human wish, desire or hope to make things better. As to what it is that requires betterment, there is little agreement. Only the desire for it seems common. Many seem not even to hope for it in this world, only in the world to come.

Some see betterment as achievable by carrying out certain rituals; some by undergoing emotional crises which they call conversion; some by professing faith in God and resolving to be amenable to His will; some by setting up five- or ten- or fifteen-year plans and working toward their achievement; some by looking toward programs for social-economic reform; some by getting more money than they now have.

Our point is that, if we can take the desire to achieve human betterment (either for ourselves or for others) as a characterization of that which we deem religious, then a religion which is nontheistic is indeed a possibility. For human sanctions can be employed in determining ways and means to achieve such a purpose as well as sanctions which are taken to be cosmic. In fact, does hard-headed examination of the events of human history show that such sanctions have ever been other than human? It is often claimed that God sanctions this or that, but each claim invariably turns out to be one made by a human being and based solely upon human conviction.

What might be the nature of a religion based on the assumption of humanly derived ideals and humanly derived truths? An ideal is something to hope for, an end or goal to attain if at all possible—or to strive toward if attainment seems impossible—a good which we would like sometime to possess. A truth is a principle which indicates the action necessary to achieve an end, a dependable means to an end.

If ideals or ends are taken as God-sanctioned, then man must not tamper with them. Therein lies sacrilege. Man has merely to determine what means are necessary for their achievement. In other words, God-sanctioned ends (which are absolute) are complete justification for any means necessary to attain them—"the ends justify the means." Need I enumerate the kinds of deeds which this principle has evoked during the course of human history?

If, on the other hand, ideals or ends are taken as man-sanctioned, then whenever man sees that certain ends are not working out as he anticipated—when he sees certain ends requiring or leading to means which seem inhumane or indecent —he has no hesitation in reconsidering his ideals or purposes to see whether indeed they are not in need of renovation.

Thus we arrive at Dewey's proposal that an act or an effort which is to be considered religious is one in which ends and means—"the ideal and the actual"—are, either or both, so modified as to be brought more nearly in keeping with one another. It may be that ideals require alteration; it may be that procedures need to be changed; or it may be that reciprocal adjustment is indicated. In any case, it is man's judgment which is the court of last resort—collective judgment, of course, whenever collective wrongs require adjudication.

And it is not a kingdom which is indicated but a democracy in which all participate on equal terms in arriving at decisions and all are equally obligated to abide by the decisions. Democratic governance is *the* means for achieving relativization of human social values. Democracy is a foe of absolutes.

Faith in Human Abilities

Thus, what is it that represents divinity if not mankind's perennial and indefatigable struggle toward something which he deems better than what he now has? And what has placed him above the beasts of the field and even the fowls of the air, making him little lower than the angels, if not a human intellect which can abstract particularized qualities from concrete situations, transfer them in imagination to other situations and thereby create something new under the sun? What higher respect can we show man than this? And, if we wish to go further and assume God to be man's creator, what more than this has been said of the greatness of God's creation?

Moreover, there is a place in a faith such as this for what, if not supernatural, is at least superindividual. That represents recognition of the oft-demonstrated principle that in union there is strength. In working together, on the basis of democratic governance and of employing the scientific way to attain truth (which is indeed a democratic way), men can and do achieve far more than any or all of them can or could possibly achieve by working each to himself alone. The idea that a group can rise no higher than its greatest member is doubtless a false one, hardly to be taken seriously by anyone who has had opportunity to witness the tremendous achievements of modern, cooperative, scientific endeavor. Yes, by working freely and amicably together, man is in a real sense able to transcend himself, to achieve superhumanity. What more is divinity?

A relativistic philosophy is one in which faith is freely and frankly placed in man himself. Man has to deal with a world which is not of his own choosing. But he does so on the basis of truths for which he himself is responsible, formulated by means of an inductive-deductive method which we call scientific, and on the basis of a value-system for which he is disposed to blame no one but himself. Whatever may be the assistance he has received from other sources, man's truth-system and value-system are taken to be his own responsibility. He may take them or leave them as he sees fit. Faith, ideals, truth and commitment all play a real part in a relativistic system of thought.

Yet, though affording man tremendous freedom in ordering his way of life, relativistic philosophy is in no wise completely subjectivistic, solipsistic or based on the doctrine of absolute free will. Dewey's perceptual principle—that what I make of the world before me has to be agreeable to that world —is a thorough denial of solipsism.

In the degree to which I enjoy freedom in concocting my truth-and-value system, to that degree do I shoulder the responsibility for adopting a truth-and-value system which is competent and noble. Competence and nobility are not forced upon me, nor is there any guarantee that I shall evince them. But when I recognize that competence and nobility will be mine only if and when I choose and achieve a way of life which will display these virtues, then I see that I must work at the job, that I must employ my own resources to their fullest, that I must be a disciplined person—one who, though taking my full measure of enjoyment of life, nevertheless must bestir myself in ways not always agreeable or enjoyable to do my just part in ordering and carrying on the affairs of the world.

Bibliography

Bayles, E. E. *Democratic Educational Theory.* New York: Harper, 1960.

Bentley, A. F. *Inquiry into Inquiries.* Boston: Beacon Press, 1954.

Bolton, C. D. "Sociological Relativism and the New Freedom," *Ethics,* 1957, 68, 11-27.

Cantril, H. *The "Why" of Man's Experience.* New York: Macmillan, 1950.

Childs, J. L. *American Pragmatism and Education.* New York: Holt, 1956.

Dewey, J. *A Common Faith.* New Haven: Yale University Press, 1934.

———, & Bentley, A. F. *Knowing and the Known.* Boston: Beacon Press, 1949.

Hook, S. (ed.). *John Dewey: Philosopher of Science and Freedom.* New York: Dial Press, 1950.

Ratner, S. "The Naturalistic Humanism of John Dewey and Arthur F. Bentley," *Humanist,* 1954, 14, 81-87.

Part III   Values

5   The Nature of Values

DONALD SNYGG

In a rapidly changing society like our own, social and economic situations never repeat themselves exactly. Every situation has something new about it. As a result, no economic or political planning is possible except as the planners have a concept of causation which enables them to make some guess about what people will do under circumstances which have never before arisen. This is true whether we are planning individually as businessmen or consumers or collectively as citizens. The faster the society changes, the more its members have to depend on theory.

One of the major obstacles in the way of getting more dependable concepts for predicting economic behavior is our limited knowledge of psychology. Economic or political behavior is behavior by people. When economists analyze and interpret economic behavior, when they forecast the outcome of this or that economic policy or trend, they are forecasting what people will do. To do this, an accurate concept of human nature is essential. Any theories or predictions about what people will do are certain to be inaccurate if they are based on false concepts of the people whose behavior is being predicted.

This places economists and other social scientists in an

awkward situation. Human beings are complex organisms and there are a great many conflicting theories about them. In choosing among these theories we cannot safely trust our limited personal experience, which may have been with a special kind of people. The social or economic theorist who bases his theories of what people will do on his personal version of human nature is quite likely to get a theory which is applicable only to his own generation of his society or to his own social class. In fact, he is in danger of getting a theory which is applicable only to himself.

If he protects himself against this provincialism by basing his economic theories on the current psychological concepts, he can still get into difficulties. The conceptual systems of professional psychologists are in the process of development and some of them, including some which psychologists are very hopeful about, are still too specialized to be applicable to the behavior of human beings outside the laboratory. The social scientist who uses a theory of this type without understanding its sources is in danger of building his picture of society on a theory which in its current incomplete form is applicable only to the maze behavior of the white rat.

And no matter which conceptual framework he adopts, he will find many of its concepts unconvincing because they are contrary to what he and his readers have always thought to be common sense.

Common-Sense Concepts of Human Nature

One of the main obstacles in the way of our learning more about human nature is the fact that we already "know"

so many things about it that are not true. Most people can recognize their ignorance of such subjects as entomology or cultural anthropology or nuclear physics, but few people except
professional psychologists feel ignorant about human nature.
Psychology, it is generally believed, is just common sense—
what everybody knows. Some may doubt that redheaded people are quick tempered, but it is generally held to be "common
sense" that *the* basic human needs are for food, shelter and
clothing; that practice makes perfect; that the way to cure
people of bad habits is to punish them. We delude ourselves,
however, when we believe that these generalizations are dependable or that we learned them by experience. "Common
sense" about human nature all too often turns out to be an
author's epigram or an academic theory, now disproved, which
was proposed so long ago that our grandparents heard about
it in time to teach it to our parents.

The fiction of economic man

One of the most prominent of the "common sense" barriers to better understanding of human nature is the widespread belief that economic motives are the only ones that matter in the economic realm. Studies of employee aspirations in
American industry do not confirm the idea that pay is the only
incentive or even the most important one. Wage incentive
systems frequently result in slow-downs by the more efficient workers, who do not wish to outproduce their associates.
Among American industrial workers, desire for group membership and approval has usually proved more potent than
desire for money when the two are in conflict.

Katona has reported that businessmen have a tendency to aim at increased volume rather than increased profits. He believes that economic motives are changing and lists, among others, professional pride and the desires for prestige, power and approbation.

Competition as a motive of behavior

Another common-sense idea which does not stand up in practice is the idea that people are inevitably competitive. It is quite true that most people measure their achievements by the achievements of their neighbors, and Katona has justifiably concluded that "the more money other people have the more a person wants." As used in many schools and factories, however, competition is a comparatively ineffective way of getting people to work harder. People do not compete actively unless they think they have a chance to win. This causes a large part of any group to withdraw from competition early. These people then exert pressure on the others to drop out of the competition with them.

In addition, more people are unwilling to compete when competing means the loss of friends, as it often does. Forced competition, in which people are obliged to compete against their friends, is a threat to the individual and therefore unpleasant. It is not surprising that workers or departments which have been involved in contests frequently drop their output to below normal as soon as the contest is over. As a rule, teachers who depend on competition as a means of motivation are able to get the majority of their students to compete only when they "choose up sides" and appeal to group loyalties.

Psychological Concepts of Human Nature

Although a great deal of progress has been made during the three-quarters of a century that psychology has been an experimental science, psychologists are continually reminded of the tentative nature of their generalizations by the fact that competent psychologists may still differ from one another in their preference among the various conceptual frameworks and types of explanation that are used. The truth is that human behavior is so manysided, so complex and so variable that there is no single point of view yet discovered by which we can understand it all. The problem is to find a point of view which will enable us to see the whole disorderly mass of phenomena in order and regularity, and, it is hoped, to make it predictable. In looking for a conceptual system which will make human behavior more understandable, present-day psychologists are following a number of different leads.

The stimulus-response approach to behavior

The most obvious approach is to attempt to explain behavior by the known principles of the physical sciences. Such a conceptual system was made quite plausible by the discovery of the reflex arc in 1832. It was discovered that the stimulation of a given nerve always resulted in the contraction of the same muscles, provided the spinal cord had been severed above the point where the nerve entered it. This fixed stimulus-response unit, which could be explained plausibly by several different principles of the physical sciences, was assumed to be the basic unit of behavior.

Following this assumption, the next problem was to discover how these fixed "basic" reflexes, which have been discovered in decorticate animals, combine and interact with one another to produce the more variable and coherent behavior which is characteristic of an undamaged organism—animal or human.

The most important difficulty confronting this conceptual model of behavior is the problem of stimulus selection. There are in any given physical situation great numbers of physical stimuli to which the organism makes no apparent response. A stimulus which sets off a response in one situation or at one time may have no effect at another time or in another situation. Or it may elicit a completely different response. And the stimulus which does elicit the response is not necessarily the strongest one in terms of physical energy.

This variability is ascribed either to changes in the conductivity of the nervous system or to tensions and imbalances in the organism which require (drive) it to behave so as to relieve them.

This latter concept has diverted the emphasis in physiologically oriented theories of motivation from the external physical stimulus which "triggers" the act to the internal conditions that determine which of the great number of potential factors present in the physical environment will be selected as the objects of the organism's behavior. A number of these conditions, personified as "drives" for food, water, avoidance of injury, rest, elimination, air and constant body temperature, have been taken over from physiology.

Since the behavior supposedly motivated by these physiological drives or "needs" is essential to the survival of the organism, they are often assumed to be the basic drives from which all other "drives" or "needs" are derived. These physiological drives, at least, operate in all living individuals. They are sometimes considered to constitute a single drive for physical survival or for homeostasis, that is, for the maintenance of the organism's physiological balance.

Homeostasis as an explanation of behavior

This is not a mere change of words. The concept of homeostasis enables us to visualize and use a completely different concept of living organisms from the machine concept of the stimulus-response theorists. It even leads to a different system of ethics.

Thinking in terms of the physics of their own day, the physiologists who a century ago adopted the reflex arc as their conceptual unit of behavior were taking a machine as their model. The motive power of their conceptual man was supplied from the outside in the form of a stimulus, i.e., a spur.

The newer concept of homeostasis, which also originated in physiology, assumes, on the other hand, that the living organism is an organized dynamic field and that, like all organized fields, it must behave so as to maintain its organization. Thus the organized nature of our behavior, the explanation of which has caused the stimulus-response theorists so much trouble, is simply an aspect of our nature as living organisms. An individual's behavior, from this point of view, is both the result of his physical organization and the means by which it is maintained.

The physiological evidence in favor of this concept is overwhelming and does not need to be given here. The essential thing is that this point of view leads us to conceive of human beings, not as passive machines which have to be pushed into action, but as living organisms actively exploring their environments for the means of maintaining their own integrity. They actively seek the satisfaction of need and, if we consider them as whole organisms, they have "free will." Choices between food and water, for instance, are determined by the physiological state of the organism itself.

All of this, so far, is completely in harmony with the known principles of physics and chemistry and fits into the present framework of the physical sciences. It is too bad that it is not quite adequate. A large part of human behavior and even some animal behavior cannot be explained by, or even reconciled with, the purely physiological needs. It is not uncommon for people to eat when they have already eaten more than they need or can comfortably contain. It is not uncommon for them to refuse food when they are starving. People drive too fast for safety, they mutilate themselves for beauty, they give their lives as heroes, as martyrs and as suicides—all activities which are hardly consonant with maintaining the physiological balance.

In a wartime experiment on the effects of semistarvation, the thirty-six men who were the subjects lost an average of 25 per cent of their body weight. With it they lost interest in almost everything but food. They dreamed of food, thought constantly about food. Life became, as one expressed it, merely "passing time from one meal to the next." Another reported: "Stayed up till 5:00 A.M. last night studying cookbooks. So absorbing I can't stay away from them."

This extreme preoccupation with food would seem at first glance to be an ideal example of the effect of an urge toward organic homeostasis. But, in spite of the fact that food could easily have been purchased or stolen, only a few of the participants violated their pledge to eat only the prescribed diet. When shopping they did not purchase the food needed by their bodies. Instead they bought cookbooks, cooking utensils, and "bargains." One man hoarded copies of *The National Geographic* magazine. Two men stole. But only one stole food. The other stole china cups. If this is homeostasis, it is not homeostasis in a purely physiological sense.

Even lower animals not infrequently show behavior which is hard to reconcile with a demand for bodily maintenance. The writer once had to remove a white rat from a laboratory activity wheel because of extreme loss of weight. She had been going without food and water in order to keep her cage mates from using the wheel. As soon as she was removed from the cage one of the other animals began behaving in the same way. Homeostasis can explain dominating behavior which results in the individual's getting more food, but when a poorly nourished animal abstains from food and water in order to dominate its cage mates, an explanation of the act as an effort to maintain a constant physiological state seems a little far-fetched.

The concept of psychological needs

One way of handling this difficulty is to postulate the existence of additional nonorganic drives or needs, usually called psychological needs. Among the psychological needs proposed by various writers are needs for activity *and* for relaxation, for security *and* for new experience, for self-assertion *and* for self-abasement, for imitativeness *and* for creative self-expression, for work *and* for leisure, for beauty *and* for practicability, for protection *and* for independence, for emotional security *and* for excitement, for superiority, for dominance, for status, for possession of children, for recognition, for achievement, for affection, for value, for ownership, for knowledge, for power, for prestige and for "value-in-general."

It should be obvious that this conceptual scheme gets into difficulties since it leads to the postulation of contradictory goals. If we are free to postulate a new psychological need to explain any act otherwise inexplicable, the list will grow and grow. As someone has said, this method could lead to the postulation of a psychological need for pumpkin pie in October.

In spite of the way this theory of mixed physiological-psychological needs frays out into confusion and conflict, it is popular at the present time. For one thing, it provides a convenient formula for explaining anything that anyone has ever done. If none of the many conflicting drives can explain an act, a new drive can easily be added to the list. But it is impossible to predict by this method what an individual is going to do because it offers us no way of knowing which of the many conflicting hypothetical drives will be operating. As a result, applied psychologists, whose planning often requires a fairly accurate prediction of what an individual will do in a particular situation, do not find it helpful.

This puts the psychologist in the same awkward position as the other social scientists. Economists and political scientists could go about their work with more confidence if the psychologists could give them a reliable psychology to work with. But the physical science methods which many psychologists have been taught to prefer are not yet adequate for predicting behavior outside the restricted conditions of the laboratory. Until the physiologists give them a better base to work on they cannot even begin to attack the problem.

In the meantime we are confronted with pressing problems of education, rehabilitation and social reconstruction, for which a better understanding of human nature is essential. Without it we cannot be sure of our techniques or our goals. It is not safe to try to fit these problems into a theoretical framework which, no matter how bright its prospects for the future, has not proved itself by success in prediction. Because they are expected to deal with human beings now and cannot wait for the physiological approaches to be perfected, many educational, clinical and social psychologists are exploring the possibilities of other points of view.

The group as a determiner of behavior

Two different and, to some extent, complementary approaches seem to be developing. The first uses the principle which Professor Emerson has rather happily called "social homeostasis." Like physical organisms and other dynamic fields, the social group exists independently of any of its individual parts. It may exist long after all of its individual parts have been replaced; in fact it may continue to exist *because* some of its parts have been discarded.

Another characteristic that human societies and living organisms share with other dynamic fields is that their response to their external environment is selective. The type of response evoked by an environmental change depends upon the nature of the society or the organism; and changes which evoke a violent response from one society will elicit no response from another.

A frequently cited example of this selectivity in the social field is Linton's study of the Tanala-Betsileo. These two Madagascar tribes apparently shared the same culture until the Betsileo shifted from dry rice culture to wet rice culture. The wet rice culture has a number of economic advantages since it gives a higher yield, provides for better conservation of the soil and can be carried out by single families. Since the system does not require frequent removal to new land it has the further advantage of enabling families engaged in wet rice culture to live in better and more permanent homes. Nevertheless, one of the Tanala clans which took up the new method soon abandoned it because it interfered with their religious ceremonies.

This same study furnishes other examples of the way in which societies function as dynamic fields. Because of the interdependent character of the organization in such a field, changes in one part of the field will affect—sometimes drastically—all other parts of the field. Once the Betsileo took up wet rice culture a profound change in their society followed. The fact that the land suitable for such cultivation was scattered in small plots which could be cultivated more or less permanently made private ownership of the land desirable. Since the cultivation was by families rather than by clans (as it had been before), the ownership was by families. Class distinctions began to appear as a result of differences in family wealth. Slaves acquired economic value. Because the limiting factor in production was water, a strong central power to control irrigation became essential. The result was that the Betsileo developed a "rigid caste system with a king at the head, nobles, commoners, and slaves." In consequence the individual Betsileo has a different style of behavior and different behavior goals from the individual Tanala.

The recent studies of social class in American communities abound with examples of the ways in which class membership helps determine the values, goals and aspirations of individual Americans. In the "Yankee City" of the early 1930s, the typical upper-upper-class member believed in heredity and manners as determinants of worth and status. He wanted money, not as an end in itself, but as a means of living "properly" in the family house, surrounded by symbols of the family position in the community, a position which it was his goal to maintain. The members of the middle class, on the other hand, believed in the power of money and education and wanted them both in order to gain higher status. The typical member of the 25 per cent of the population who constituted the lower lower class cared little for education and looked on money as something to be spent for immediate satisfactions. These three social classes thus seem to obey different laws of economics.

Man is fundamentally a social animal. As an isolated individual he does not amount to much and he seems to know it. In spite of the accusations often made that the group holds its members back from progress and self-fulfillment, the truth is that, whatever our role, we can achieve it only in cooperation with others. Lewin demonstrated that people change their ways of living faster in groups than they can individually. They also seem to think more effectively when they do it together. In one experiment Shaw gave three reasoning problems to each of twenty-one individuals and to five groups of four people each. The individuals, working alone, arrived at correct solutions to only 8 per cent of the problems, the groups to 56 per cent.

The effect of group membership on behavior in schools and factories has already been mentioned. If we want to predict what a person will probably do in a given situation, the fastest way is to find out what groups he feels part of and what his role is in the groups.

Inadequacies of social group theories

And yet the assumption that an individual behaves as he does because he is a member of a group which requires such behavior leaves a great many questions unanswered. Suppose that a man is a member of many different groups, as most people are nowadays. If the interests of these groups conflict, what will he do? The group-determinant hypothesis cannot tell us.

It is necessary to distinguish, at this point, between the rough hypothesis that the behavior of an individual will be that which is required by his social role and the more sophisticated principle of social homeostasis advanced by Professor Emerson. In a static society like that of the social insects the difference can be ignored. The fact that a society has existed unchanged for a reasonable period of time indicates that it has developed the techniques necessary for its survival. As long as its environment remains unchanged such a society will continue to maintain itself, provided that its members continue to play their required roles. But in human societies, even the most ancient of which are now being forced into constant change by the changes in their social and physical surroundings, the survival of the society is often possible only if the members break out of the traditional patterns and abandon their old roles for new ones.

This places us in an uncomfortable dilemma. If we follow the social role hypothesis we are unable to explain social change or to predict its course or even its direction because social change requires a change in roles, which the group theory does not explain. If we adopt the more subtle and inspiring concept of social homeostasis we cannot explain why some societies and groups fail to make the changes required for successful self-maintenance. Neither concept gives us much help in predicting the behavior of specific persons. Neither one explains why new groups are formed or what happens in situations which the social sanctions do not cover. They do not explain why some people disregard the sanctions of their native society to identify with and accept the sanctions of another.

Effective as they may be for other purposes, it does not seem that any of the psychological approaches we have described so far can give a clear picture of human purpose or human value. The physiological theories seem to imply that a society is good to the extent that it produces and distributes the goods necessary for the physical health of its members; but the fact that "psychological" needs have to be invoked to supplement the purely physiological needs indicates that people need something more than the physical necessities of life. It is hard to say just what this is, because the alleged psychological needs are so diverse and conflicting.

The social-determinant theories of behavior give a picture of value which is even more disconcerting because they seem to disregard completely the fate of the individual human being. The successful society, this approach implies, is the society which survives. Whether or not this society satisfies the need or helps fulfill the destiny of human beings in general or of specific persons in particular is not pertinent to this point of view. It is reasonable to suppose that societies will have better chances for survival if their institutions and customs tend to keep their members alive, maintain their loyalty and attract new adherents. In other words, the successful society must to some extent satisfy human need. But by itself the group approach, whose basic dynamism is the maintenance and extension of the group organization, gives us no inkling about what people need. The basic problem which must be solved before we can understand group dynamics thus turns out to be the problem of basic human values. What is the motivating purpose of human behavior?

The Individual-Field Approach

At the present time a number of psychologists appear to be more or less independently converging on a purely psychological theory of behavior which is more capable of dealing with the problems of human purpose and human values than the physiological and group approaches we have already discussed. These people do not form a school or group and do not share a formally organized body of theory, so that what follows is only my personal analysis of the general approach. The basic postulates appear to be these:

1. *The behavior of human beings is always appropriate to what is variously called the individual's psychological field, behavioral field, private world, assumptive world, perceptual field or phenomenal field.*

This is the crucial assumption of the approach. Instead of abandoning field dynamics because in the guise of organic homeostasis it is not adequate to explain all behavior, the individual-field psychologists keep the principle and move it to a conceptual causal field where it does work.

In terms of what we know about living organisms, some such field is biologically necessary to animals with distance perception. Among those animals which remain small and live in the water or in a host organism, getting their food by drifting into contact with it or having it drift into contact with them, behavior is purely homeostatic. The only part of the physical environment which affects the animal or its behavior is that part which is in close contact with its surface. Such an animal lives in a behavioral field one molecule thick, and anything nutritive or noxious within that area is automatically dealt with. The individual has no choice of action and all animals of the species would respond in the same way.

An animal of this kind is unable to perceive food at a distance and move toward it, or to perceive danger at a distance and avoid it. It is completely at the mercy of its environment. If such a species is to survive, one of two things has to happen. As one alternative its individual members might develop a high rate of reproduction and enough motility to scatter them so widely that a few, at least, would always be blundering into a favorable environment. Or, after developing motility, the individual organism might increase its chances for survival by developing distance perception so that it could perceive food or danger at a distance and behave accordingly.

But this presents a new problem. An animal able to perceive objects at a distance is now exposed to stimuli from a tremendous number of food and danger foci. An organism which responded simultaneously to all of the physical stimuli which bombard it from these sources would tear itself to pieces. In order to maintain its organization it must trim the confusing, stunning, incoherent field with which it is now in contact down to manageable size. *It has to pick out that part of the physical field which is most important to the mainte-nance of its own organization at the moment and deal with that,* more or less ignoring the rest. (A man being chased by a bull cannot afford to notice the mosquitoes.) This "cut-down" field is the individual, or psychological, field.

One important feature of the "cut-down" psychological field is that it has a *time dimension.* It includes a past and a future. For the organism whose behavioral world is limited to its immediate surface, nothing exists except what is here and now, but the acquisition of distance perception automatically gives the field a time dimension. Food at a distance is not, for the organism, food now. If it is perceived at all as food it is "food-in-the-future."

As a result of this development, great individual differ-ences and apparent irrationalities in behavior begin to appear. The degree of choice required by the simplest type of distance perception results in wide differences between individual fields of different individuals in the same physical situation.[1] And when an organism like man is able to symbolize and introduce into its psychological field objects and concepts not physically

---

[1] The irrationalities are only apparent. Behavior is judged irrational when it is not appropriate to the perceptual field of the observer. The sequence of plays chosen by a quarterback who is trying to coax the defense out of position to set up a breakaway play for a touchdown will appear foolish to a spectator who sees the situation in a shorter time perspective and thinks only in terms of maximum gain on the next down. And the spectator's choices would appear irrational to the quarter-back.

present, the range of possible behavior becomes tremendous. The behavior of individuals would be completely unpredictable if it were not for the next principle.

2. *The psychological field is an organized dynamic field.* The immediate purpose of all of an individual's behavior, including his behavior as a perceiver, is the maintenance of organization in his individual field. If the field organization should disintegrate, his physical organization could not be maintained. If he loses faith in his perceptions, organized behavior becomes impossible.

Seasickness is an illustration of the breakdown of physical organization which occurs in a disorganized perceptual field. Workers at the Hanover Institute report that subjects exposed to perceptual phenomena which they are unable to reconcile with one another frequently become nauseated.

3. *The meaning and value of perceived objects and events are determined by the individual's field organization at the time.* As examples we can take the different meaning and value to an individual of food before and after a heavy meal. Our perceptions seem to follow dynamic-field principles in that events and objects are always interpreted in the way which will require the least change in the field. Suppose, for instance, that a large part of my perceptual field is organized around the belief that a certain man is an enemy. Then, on an important occasion, he treats me with kindness and generosity. The odds are that I will perceive his behavior as a subtle insult or a deliberate attempt to deceive. If he were unimportant to me, I would be able to change my perception of him as a result of his kind act. But since his supposed enmity plays an important role in my field organization, it will be easier to distort my perception of his act than to change the rest of my field to conform

to the act. Many of the demonstrations devised by Ames and his associates at the Hanover Institute illustrate this principle.

4. *The perceptual self is the part of the field which is perceived as behaving. As a result it is the focal part of the field.* The only aspects of the cosmos which seem important, indeed the only aspects which can enter the field at all, are those which are related to the self. If the principle of field organization is too abstract to be useful, we can paraphrase it by saying that the immediate purpose of all behavior is the maintenance of the behaver's perceptual field, particularly of his perceptual self.

This takes care of the problems of martyrdom and suicide—inexplicable by physiological principles and, in the case of suicide in our society, where it is socially disapproved, by the concept of group role. It is not the physical self but *the self-as-perceived*, the perceptual self, which we are trying to preserve. A man who has come to think of himself as selfless and devoted to duty or to others will act so as to maintain that perception of himself, even at the expense of his life. There are strong connotations for character education here. A person who has been taught to perceive himself as an outsider will behave like an outsider, with no feeling of responsibility to the group. A person who has been taught to regard himself as a criminal has to maintain and enhance that concept of himself by believing that "only suckers work."

5. *Because human beings are aware of the future, at least of its existence and uncertainties, it is not enough to maintain the perceptual self for the present moment.* It has to be maintained in the future, built up and enhanced so that the individual feels secure for the future. And since the future is uncertain and unknown, no enhancement of the individual's experi-

ence of personal value, no degree of self-actualization, is enough. Human beings are, by nature, insatiable.

The ideal sought is a state in which the individual feels so much in harmony with the universe, so much a part of it, that he does not have to defend himself against any other part. It is interesting that this state is said to have been achieved, at least in moments of ecstasy, by some of the saints. The experience probably involves a perception of the universe as pervaded with infinite love and compassion for all living things.

Ways of satisfying need

Seen in this way, the many conflicting physiological and psychological "needs" which were discussed earlier turn out to be alternative ways of satisfying the individual's basic need for enhancement of his experience of personal worth and value. A more convenient classification of these alternative ways of satisfying need follows. Since behavior is always determined by the individual field of the behaver, the method used by any individual in any situation will be one which is appropriate to his perceptions of himself and of the external situation at that particular time.

Means of Maintaining and Enhancing the Self

A. Change in body state leading to change in the perceptions of the self.
  1. Restoration of the body balance by eating, breathing, elimination, rest, etc.
  2. Blocking off organic sensations of fatigue, pain or tensions indicative of personal inadequacies by the use of alcohol or drugs.

    3. Elicitation of an organic mobilization and increase in body strength by entering a dangerous or irritating situation: speeding, gambling, etc.

B. Self-reassurance by demonstration of mastery, control or superiority.

    1. Over people. Competition leading to victory over worthy opposition. Other demonstrations of superiority by gossip, practical joking, scapegoating, making gifts, etc.

    2. Over material objects. Creative activities (doodling to art) or destructive activities (nail-biting to vandalism). Accumulation of property, hoarding behavior.

C. Reassurance and enhancement by association and identification with respected individuals and groups.

    1. Evidence of respect and love by respected persons.

    2. Feeling of identity with a great cause, or being part of a great movement.

D. Change in the nonself part of the field which places the self in a less threatened position.

    1. Change in the physical environment. Travel, moving, redecorating, etc.

    2. Daydreaming or fantasy, including that done by professionals. Radio, television, theater, fiction, etc.

Creative activities provide more permanent symbols of self-value than destructive activities, but they usually take longer and require more skill. Destructive acts therefore are more apt to be committed by an immature person or a person under great stress, provided that they are not inconsistent with the perceptual self he is trying to enhance.

Many activities help to satisfy the need for enhancement in several ways. The most satisfying sex experiences associate means A and C. Cigarette smoking, particularly for smokers who inhale, supplies a tissue irritant which causes a rise in blood pressure and an increase in heartbeat and amount of blood sugar (A_2 and A_3). The smoker also secures reassurance from manipulating an object and blowing smoke (B_2). (Many smokers report that they get less pleasure from smoking in the dark.) He may also use smoking as a way of demonstrating membership in social groups (C) and gain a feeling of value by offering cigarettes and matches to people without them. It is small wonder that many millions of dollars a year are spent for tobacco and that the statistics on lung cancer have not had a drastic effect on its consumption.

The basis of human values

Looking at the problem of value from this point of view we can come to the following conclusions:

1. The basic goal of all individuals is for a feeling of increased worth, of greater value.

2. This goal is never completely reached. Given one success, one degree of self-enhancement, human beings will always aspire to more.

3. Satisfaction of the need for greater personal value can be and is sought in a number of alternative ways. Goods and experiences are of value to the individual only as they contribute to the feeling of personal worth.

We are now in a position to make some judgments about values. Since the individual can strive, with some success, for

self-enhancement in a number of different ways, no single
way is indispensable.[2]

The Special Status of Economic Activity

Although economic activity is only one of many ways
by which the individual strives for an increased feeling of
worth, value and belonging, it is likely to demand a major portion of his time and attention. Economic activity takes a great
deal of time because it is concerned with the control of
"scarce" goods, that is, with materials and services that require
conscious effort to get. Many of the scarce materials would
be helpful to their possessor even if they were not scarce. Food
and clothing, for instance, may be used to maintain or restore
the body balance and increase the consumer's perception of
body strength. An automobile may be used to increase the
driver's feeling of power and value, by helping him to earn his
living or by giving him a chance to exhibit skill and good judgment or daring.

But objects or services do not have to be useful in such a
direct fashion to be valuable. Scarcity alone can make an object valuable because the mere possession of a scarce object,
provided it is sought by others, can be a constant and reassuring symbol of dignity, worth and power. Air is necessary for
self-maintenance but no one will derive the fullest possible

[2] The only qualification is that if the individual fails to use the
methods for seeking enhancement which also result in maintaining the
body balance, he will die. As a usual thing he will use such methods
because any marked physical disorganization results in such a change
in the psychological field that the individual does act so as to restore
the body balance. But this is not always the case.

satisfaction from air until it is bottled under expensive brand names and sold at such high prices that the consumers (and hoarders) are impressed by their own wealth, extravagance and good taste. As things stand now we do a great deal of breathing but devote little attention to it. Since air is not scarce, breathing ordinarily presents no problems and therefore no opportunity for self-enhancement by overcoming obstacles.

At a social level in which the minimal physical necessities are so easily obtained that their possession arouses no pride, a great deal of time may be devoted to the economic struggle for such symbols of worth as modern kitchen equipment, antique (or ultramodern) furniture, mink coats or a private office with its own water cooler—all of which would lose much of their value if they became more plentiful or if people quit competing for them. As long as such objects are scarce, it takes quite a bit of effort and ability or power to get them. As a result, they have come to be, in the eyes of many, reassuring symbols of self-worth and status. Such people will sacrifice a great deal to get them.

Superficially each individual has a large number of alternative symbolic goals available, but actually he can strive with hope and satisfaction only for the goals which are appropriate to his concept of himself and the situation. Failure to achieve the goals by which he has chosen to measure himself results in humiliation and anguish. And these feelings are not lessened by his power to achieve other ends which are not appropriate to his self concept and are therefore not regarded as enhancing.

The value transaction

This point of view, if it should come to be accepted as common sense, would lead to a better appreciation of the role played by the businessman in the production of values. It is sometimes assumed that value is an intrinsic property of the object and that anyone who buys an object for less than that value gets a bargain and anyone who pays more is a loser. This leads to the belief that neither the buyer nor the seller has produced anything. A business transaction, from this point of view, is a contest between two parties each of whom is trying to victimize the other by buying goods for less or selling them for more than their intrinsic worth. From this point of view business is attempted cheating and the model transaction is the purchase of Manhattan Island from the Indians.

From the individual-field point of view, however, both parties to a transaction may, and usually do, profit from it. Objects are valuable to people if they assist them in the satisfaction of their individual need for self-maintenance and enhancement. Since different people strive for satisfaction of this need in different ways, objects and experiences will have different values for different people, and both parties to an exchange which is free from coercion can be expected to profit by it. A model transaction, from this point of view, might be one between a starving man with a keg of water and a man suffering from thirst who has a surplus of food.

The process of choice

This approach also provides a conceptual framework for dealing with the process of choice. Lacking such a framework, economists have had to assume that anyone's choice of goals is perfectly free, limited only by the possibilities of the physical environment. In any actual situation the choice is much more narrowly limited, since, in order to be chosen, an object or experience has to be perceived as a means by which the individual can approach closer to his goal. What will be chosen is thus determined by the nature and organization of the chooser's field at the instant of choice. People in the same physical situation will make different choices because they have different goals, or because they are in different stages of their progress toward their goals or for a number of other reasons. A person under strong pressure, for instance, is likely to concentrate so strongly on his immediate goal that he will fail to perceive opportunities to bypass it when they occur. When he feels threatened by intense and immediate loss of self-respect, the future aspects of his private field fade into the background and he acts "without foresight."

There is reason to believe that what people call "foresight" is related to the individual's concept of himself. The person who feels relatively secure in his feelings of personal worth does not need to concentrate so completely on the immediate problem and therefore has a better chance to see it in a broad perspective.

All of this seems to negate another assumption frequently made by economists, which is that the chooser is a completely rational and highly informed being capable of action in his own best interests.

Self-Interest and Altruism

The fact that man is potentially able to strive for satisfaction of need in many different ways gives us an answer to
an important question, which may be stated in two different
ways: "Is man naturally good or evil?" or "Is man essentially
altruistic or essentially selfish?"

Since we believe that a man's behavior may be either
good or evil, it seems to follow that a good society will help
and encourage him to strive for enhancement in ways which
further not only his own experience of personal value but the
value experiences of others as well. The self-enhancement
which accrues from an experience of being needed, from feeling part of a great movement, from contributing to something
nobler and more important than our own lives, is just as natural
and probably more lasting than the self-enhancement gained
through successful aggression. In the long run it is better for
the individual himself if he uses the socially desirable ways of
seeking enhancement because such methods are not so apt to
incite other people to thwart and resist him. There is no necessary conflict between the basic aspirations of the individual
and the basic aspiration of others. There is no inevitable conflict between the individual and society.

Failure of identification with others

Let us consider, however, one way in which man may fall
into anti-human behavior. The person who does not feel part
of a social group will not behave as a member of the group.

Even though a concept of himself as a just or honorable man may keep him from consciously self-seeking behavior at the expense of the people with whom he does not identify, his feelings and, as a result, his behavior toward them will be essentially selfish. Since the organization of our individual field is largely determined by our own need for a feeling of self-worth, it is easy for such a "good citizen" who does not feel one with his victims to commit great acts of aggression against people "for their own good" or in the name of justice, of patriotism, of economic law or of preservation of the faith, and to do it in all sincerity and with a great feeling of rectitude.

Law and ethics can help prevent injustice that we can recognize, but the best insurance against injustice is complete identification with the potential victim so that injury to the victim is injury to the self. The man who loves his neighbor as himself has not abandoned self-interest. He still seeks for self-maintenance and enhancement, but now his self includes his neighbor.

Identification as the basis of ethics

It is on this base that human ethics seem to have developed best. It is true that on logical grounds it is to almost everyone's advantage to work together on the basis of "You scratch my back and I'll scratch yours." But attempts to explain existing systems of ethics or to create new ones on the basis of enlightened self-interest seem to be psychologically unrealistic. For a society to survive it must receive from some of its members sacrifices, sometimes of their lives, for which it cannot compensate them in a material sense. A system of ethics based on *quid pro quo* could in no way command the degree of self-sacrifice required and secured in all societies. This self-sacrifice seems to be a manifestation of identification, love, and faith in something more important than our own lives.

There is a growing feeling among psychologists that self-acceptance is necessary before we can accept or love others. Rogers has concluded on the basis of his clinical experience and research that a person who feels so threatened that he is preoccupied with the necessity for defending himself has little sympathy to give to others.

The degree to which men can attain brotherhood with all men is still unknown. Professor Emerson, looking at the problem against the background of millions of years of biological development, sees it as a goal which is almost assured. From a psychological point of view it does not seem impossible, given enough time. Man is certainly not averse to identifying himself with others. But he tends to identify most completely with comparatively small groups, probably because he can more clearly perceive his value to such a group.

The greatest obstacle in the way of universal brotherhood at the present time is *not* man's unregenerate selfishness and individualism. It is the fact that in order to give their lives meaning and dignity the people of the world have identified themselves with a great number of conflicting groups and causes for which many of them are prepared to sacrifice themselves *and others*.

Limitations of individual experience

It is not yet safe to assume that the process of identification with larger and larger groups can go on indefinitely. The individual field is at best only a limited version of reality, and as the group becomes larger and more complex it is more and more difficult for the individual to perceive his value and function in it and consequently to seek identification with it. Education can help, but no matter how highly educated we are, there are physiological and psychological limits to our ability to comprehend and identify with a complex society—and many people in our society may already have approached those limits. There is something suspicious about the way one civilization after another goes into a decline after it gets to the point where there is a high degree of interdependence between people who are not personally acquainted.

Even if we should succeed in getting a better conception of our relation to others, the resulting feeling of brotherhood might be disappointingly mild. The "cut-down" nature of the perceptual field makes it impossible for us ever to achieve as warm a feeling of identification with all as we now have with some. The more people we identify with, the less time and interest we can give to each. It may follow that a man who loves all of mankind equally will not love any one person much.

The Good Society

Since there are many ways in which people can secure some degree of self-actualization, it is reasonable to suppose that there can be many different "good" societies. However, if we judge a society by its contribution to the value experience of individual human beings, a society is good to the extent that it enables its members and neighbors to live with health, security, self-respect and dignity. It is good to the extent that it enables its members and neighbors to feel adequate to live with reality and, in consequence, to perceive it without distortion. Such a society will institutionalize and encourage techniques of production and cooperation among its members. Each person will have an opportunity to work, to be successful and to feel that his life has meaning and importance.

A society which is focused on human fulfillment will, by necessity, be continually changing. No successes and no recognition can be enough to give anyone the permanent feeling of adequacy and self-assurance that he requires. Further achievement and growth are always necessary. As a result, no society which attempts to remain static can adequately satisfy the needs of its members. A "good society" must provide its members with opportunities for self-enhancement by pioneering in new fields and undertaking ever more difficult problems.

Bibliography

Cantril, H. *The "Why" of Man's Experience.* New York: Macmillan, 1950.

Emerson, A. E. "The Biological Foundations of Ethics and Social Progress." In A. D. Ward (ed.), *Goals of Economic Life.* New York: Harper, 1953. Pp. 277-304.

Frank, L. K. *Nature and Human Nature.* New Brunswick: Rutgers University Press, 1951.

Guetzkow, H. S., and Bowman, P. H. *Men and Hunger.* Elgin, Ill.: Brethren Publishing House, 1946.

Ittelson, W. H. *The Ames Demonstrations in Perception.* Princeton: Princeton University Press, 1952.

Katona, G. *Psychological Analysis of Economic Behavior.* New York: McGraw-Hill, 1951.

Kuenzli, A. E. (ed.). *The Phenomenological Problem*. New York: Harper, 1959.

Lewin, K. "Group Decision and Social Change." In T. Newcomb & E. L. Hartley (eds.), *Readings in Social Psychology*. New York: Holt, 1947. Pp. 330-344.

Linton, R. "The Change from Dry to Wet Rice Cultivation in Tanala-Betsileo." In T. Newcomb & E. L. Hartley (eds.), *Readings in Social Psychology*. New York: Holt, 1947. Pp. 46-51.

Moloney, J. C. "A String of Fish," *Humanist*, 1956, 16, 162-166.

Rogers, C. R. *Client-centered Therapy*. Boston: Houghton Mifflin, 1951.

Shaw, M. E. "A Comparison of Individuals and Small Groups in the Rational Solution of Complex Problems." In T. Newcomb & E. L. Hartley (eds.), *Readings in Social Psychology*. New York: Holt, 1947. Pp. 304-315.

Snygg, D., and Combs, A. W. *Individual Behavior*. New York: Harper, 1949. Rev. ed., 1959.

Warner, W. L., and Lunt, P. S. *The Social Life of a Modern Community*. New Haven: Yale University Press, 1941.

6   A Naturalistic Ethics

Y. H. KRIKORIAN

In the last hundred years or so, great changes have taken place in our conception of the physical world, of man and society, as well as in our patterns of living. The theory of organic evolution, by establishing continuity between man and other living beings, has shown him to be a product of nature. Social and cultural researches, by uncovering a large variety of culture patterns, have given a clearer account of the structure of society. At the turn of the century, relativity and quantum theories provided us with a new picture of nature. Equally striking have been the changes in our mode of living. Technology and industrialization have imposed new shapes on our civilization. There has been an intense urbanization and a consequent change in community and family life.

John Dewey, who was born in the year Darwin's *Origin of Species* was first published, passed through all these changes and his philosophy was shaped by the demands and conflicts that resulted from them. Philosophy, if it is to be significant in a culture, has to deal with the important issues of that culture. The major conflict that characterizes our civilization, as Dewey has persistently maintained, is between the growing power of science and technology on the one hand and the lagging moral attitudes and social institutions on the other. Traditional morality, with its pre-scientific attitude, is still a pervasive factor but is out of harmony with the demands of contemporary life. Science has established continuity between man and nature but the older morality is still based on extranatural sanctions. Science insists on observation and experiment to solve our problems but the older morality demands fixed standards or imperatives. Technology and industry have rendered obsolete institutions to which the older morality still clings. There is a sharp dualism within our civilization; how shall we resolve it?

Empiricism in Ethics

Dewey deals boldly with this cleavage between science and traditional morality. His central thesis is that it must be overcome by naturalizing ethics: by placing man in nature, by determining moral values and standards in terms of human experience and, above all, by using the experimental method in dealing with ethical problems. To naturalize ethics is to change it into an empirical enterprise. But this process does not mean for Dewey, as is sometimes believed, that the ideal aspects of life should be disregarded or belittled; what it does mean is that continuity must be established between them and the natural conditions of life.

Dewey's naturalistic ethics, in its broad outline, is clear and impressive but many of its details are open to controversy. His analysis is not always easy to follow and some of his arguments are involved and seamless. But for the present we should not be diverted from the broad aspects of his ethics, which constitute a major philosophic contribution to our era.

Ethics is concerned with human conduct. On the whole this concern has two aspects—or differences in emphasis. One of them has been the formulation of rules or imperatives to check desires or impulses. In this sense, ethics is primarily a matter of what one should not do or of what negative commandments one should obey. Yet, in its positive sense, ethics is less interested in such prohibitions than in discovering and realizing ends or values, the object being to make of life a worthwhile experience. Dewey has always emphasized this positive aspect. As far back as his *The Study of Ethics: A Syllabus*, written in 1894, he expressed his conviction that amid the prevalence of "pathological and moralistic ethics, there is room for a theory which conceives of conduct as the normal and free living of life as it is." From this standpoint the task of ethics resolves itself into one major inquiry: the search for the nature of human good. Dewey's ethics in this positive sense involves many important ideas. I shall consider some of the more distinctive ones.

The Concept of Value

First, if ethics is concerned with the good, we should try to understand what Dewey means by the term "good," or rather by the term "value," the latter being more commonly used in contemporary philosophic discussions. Value is a central idea in ethics. Such terms as "good and bad," "right and wrong," "justice and injustice" and "the highest good" involve the concept of value. Some find the source and meaning of value, especially when the adjective "higher" is added, in some extra-empirical realm or notion, like divine authority or an a priori absolute; others find the source and meaning of value in natural, human experience. Dewey's view of value is of the latter kind.

Usually those who claim that the source and meaning of value reside in human experience identify it with desire or interest. "Value consists," writes a contemporary philosopher, "in the fulfillment of an interest as such"; and by interest is meant "a subject's liking or disliking." Cigarettes have value for those who like smoking; music, for the lovers of music; power, for ambitious men. This view has been effectively defended by Santayana, Russell and especially by Perry, whose words I have just quoted.

To a certain extent, Dewey agrees with this standpoint since it connects values with concrete human experiences and satisfactions and thus avoids the pallid remoteness of purely rationalistic or nonempirical approaches. Yet he finds the formulation limited and inadequate. For Dewey, if desire is to yield a meaningful notion of value, one must introduce a judgment, a comparison or an appraisal. What he is insisting upon may be illustrated by the difference between desire and the desirable, between satisfaction and the satisfactory, between liking and the likable. In the second member of each pair the notion of estimation, criticism, appraisal is involved, so that desire or liking has acquired new properties.

Valuation, from this standpoint, is concerned with the means-consequence relation. In this sense medicine is good for the patient, and a car for one who intends to travel. Moreover, valuation as appraisal is *a prescription*, not merely a description, of fact. When a doctor tells a patient that a certain way of living is good for his recovery, he is not merely stating a fact but giving a rule—which the patient must follow to regain his health. Finally, and this is important for Dewey, appraisals and judgments of value are open to empirical verification. The doctor's prescription is not something purely personal; it is based on the facts of the situation.

The Meaning of Morality

If value is what is appraised, the transition to ethical value is a natural and an important one. Many values are amoral. When one says this pen is good, this musical piece is pleasant, a summer vacation on the seashore is better than one in the mountains, one has no moral question in mind. Morality deals only with certain types of value, those designated by "right" or "wrong." What is the meaning of these ethical terms?

Dewey's analysis of ethical value is not as incisive as his notion of value in general. In reading some of his writings one gets the impression that there is no difference between value judgment and ethical judgment. Yet when Dewey's ethics is considered in its broader setting, he does make a distinction. Whenever "alternative possibilities" or "better-or-worse" qualities have important social, human consequences, they attain moral quality. He sees the distinction between value and ethical value as a matter of degree—of the importance of alternative actions to human, social interrelations—rather than a matter of difference in kind. In this sense, as Dewey rightly argues, any act may attain moral quality. Walking in itself is a trivial, amoral event but if it involves going at some risk to another's aid it may take on a moral meaning.

More precisely stated, morality is concerned with conflicting desires which "promise opposed goods" and "incompatible courses of action" in relation to their effect upon human interests and social relationships. The consequences involved in "incompatible courses of action" may be rather limited, as when the use of one's money is concerned; or they may be of worldwide importance, as when the use of the atomic bomb is concerned. The task of morality is to examine critically the consequences of alternative actions, to appraise them, in some cases to suggest a new alternative action, and finally to resolve the conflict through thought in such a way that the result will be beneficial to both the individual and society. Morally this result will be the right one, the one that *ought* to be. And "thought" here should not be taken in the rationalistic sense of apprehending certain nonempirical moral truths, but instead in the experimental sense of finding ways and means to solve the given problem.

Another important aspect of Dewey's ethics is his treatment of moral standards or ideals. The traditional moralist finds his standards already fashioned for him and sanctioned under such pretentious titles as "the moral law," "the moral order," "the wisdom of the Fathers." These absolutes are to be regarded less as means of solving behavior problems than as symbols to revere, to be loyal to. Moral experience, as Dewey sees it, is not movement toward some well-defined and fixed goal which authority or reason can formulate in the form of universal maxims or categorical imperatives; rather it continually feels its way toward fresh sources of insight in order to exploit the potentialities of life. In this process, moral standards should be regarded as hypotheses to be verified by experience, as instruments to guide us in our attempt to keep pace with expanding knowledge and opportunities.

The Ethics of Growth

Dewey has been criticized for the relativistic implications of his ethics, and some of his sayings might justifiably provoke such criticism. But what he is primarily concerned with is that moral ideals should be allowed to grow and not be frozen into fixed, authoritarian rigidity. Even such a fruitful ideal as liberty, unless modified in its meaning and application in relation to concrete circumstances, may cease to be an agent in the beneficial shaping of experience.

Nevertheless, Dewey's ethics does contain a near-absolute standard for conduct. It is *growth*, growth of the individual and especially of society. "Growth itself," he writes, "is the only moral 'end.'" He pitches aspiration high: "Nothing but the best, the richest and fullest experience possible, is good enough for man."

Growth or progress thus means increase of rich meanings, especially in present experience, and this increase is in all dimensions—finer sensory distinctions, harmony and unification. Therefore Dewey's categorical imperative is this: "So act as to increase the meaning of present experience." Ultimately, it is in terms of this imperative that acts have to be determined as good or bad, right or wrong. A major consequence of the identification of moral ideals with growth is

the need to supplement the narrow, self-centered individualism of the past with a new social conception of individuality,
an individuality consonant with the industrial conditions under
which we live.

But even this inclusive ideal of growth should not be
mistaken for a fixed absolute and thus be changed to a sterile
standard. To achieve the more richly informed concrete qualities of experience one should steer clear of abstractions and
carefully study the specific needs and alternative possibilities
within a localized situation. "Till men give up the search for
a general formula of progress they will not know where to
look to find it."

Realization of the Good

There is a final question to be considered. How will human good and satisfaction be realized? Here we come to
Dewey's idea of the relation of means to ends in ethics. Dewey
has tirelessly insisted on the importance of this relation. He is
eager to make ideal possibilities actualities, and the method he
suggests is the determination of the true relation between
means and ends.

For Dewey, means and ends form a continuum. Ends—
or, better, ends-in-view—are the construction of *a series of
means*. Apart from means, ends have no basis. Anyone genuinely interested in an end, such as becoming a musician, must
be affectionately concerned with the means of achieving this
end—that is, with a knowledge of musical pieces and instruments and with the requisite techniques. Moreover, in the
continuum of means and ends, means are ends for the time be-

ing, and ends are means for new ends-in-view. The relation of means to ends is a continuous process in life; the distinction between them is purely relative.

The final character of an accomplished moral act depends on the character of the means used; the end is really the summation of the series of means. A democratic ideal cannot be attained by non- or antidemocratic means, since the democratic way of life is means and end in their continuous interrelation. A moral society cannot be constructed on the basis of immoral means. Thus morality applies to means as well as to ends, to the various parts of our activity as well as to the activity as a whole.

Moreover, if means and ends are internally related, then the reconstruction of morals must lean heavily on the sciences, especially on the social sciences. Intelligent formulation of morals in sex, business, politics and international relations depends heavily on the specific empirical facts in these areas. Without these facts and their use, morals in such fields are sentimental. The sharp separation between means and ends, between material conditions and ideal ends, between science and morals, must cease. Apart from material conditions, ideals are merely ineffective aspirations; apart from ideal ends, material activities tend to become narrow and harsh.

The central theme that runs through Dewey's analysis of means and ends, and through all his ethical discussion, is the belief that intelligence expressed through the experimental method should be applied to moral problems and conflicts. Whether this method will succeed where the traditional methods of authoritarianism and absolutism have failed is itself an experimental question, but it is an adventure supremely worth undertaking.

Dewey's ethical system forms a coherent, comprehensive and vitally effective whole based on the facts of life and the possibilities of experience; yet this ethics may be enlarged in certain directions within the framework of his experimental philosophy.

It should be noted that, despite his thoroughgoing empiricism, Dewey has not given sufficient consideration to the empirical question of the *content* of moral ideals. Pragmatically it is of great importance to enrich the content of desirable moral ends since the richer they are the more effective they will be in conduct. What type of individual life, family relations, economic and political institutions is most desirable, not only in terms of general principles but in a more or less detailed form?

A naturalistic ethics, if it is to be a genuine alternative to the traditional systems, cannot ignore this phase of morality. The suggestion is not to reinstate what Dewey rightly decries —the authoritative setting up of ideals for conduct prior to experience. What is being maintained is that certain large, desirable ends may be tentatively formulated and evaluated before dealing with specific situations. It is not enough to know *how* to do things; it is equally important to have some idea of *what* we want to do. The relatively concrete content of ideals must therefore become the concern of ethics. Of course, as Dewey maintains, the ideal ends should be plastic and progressively defined in terms of the conflicts and obstacles involved and of the means that are available.

The Problem of the Tragic

Moreover, Dewey has not troubled himself to show the application of intelligence to a certain area of experience: the tragic, hopeless, insoluble predicaments of life. Dewey is so passionately concerned with the possible growth of human life that he has neglected to comment on the significance of resignation and equanimity. These, too, are the fruits of intelligence. Dewey's moral attitude is not unlike Spinoza's famous saying: "A free man thinks of nothing less than of death, and his wisdom is not a meditation upon death but upon life." It is true that the energy we have should be spent more for the enhancement of life than for the discipline of facing defeat, yet no philosophy of human conduct is complete until it acknowledges the darker aspects of life and indicates attitudes that are relevant to them.

The suggestions made here both as to the pragmatic preliminary enrichment of ideal content and of the constructive role of resignation or equanimity in a dominantly active life can be incorporated into the body of Dewey's ethics. The very fact that his ethics can thus be further developed is a sign of its intrinsic fertility.

In its fundamentals Dewey's ethical theory is one of the most vital and relevant philosophies of conduct in contemporary thought. Grounded in human experience and natural events, it is an ethics exhilaratingly free from extra-empirical or supernaturalistic dogmas. Insisting on the application of experimental method or creative intelligence, it is an ethics as much opposed to the policy of listless drifting as to every kind of harsh authoritarianism. Finally, it is an ethics that is not satisfied with what is barely good enough for human beings, but demands the richest possible experience of which they are capable.

Bibliography

Burkhardt, F. (ed.). *The Cleavage in Our Culture*. Boston: Beacon Press, 1952.

Dewey, J. *Experience and Nature*. Rev. ed. New York: Norton, 1929.

———. *Human Nature and Conduct*. New York: Modern Library, 1930.

———. *A Common Faith*. New Haven: Yale University Press, 1934.

———. *Reconstruction in Philosophy*. Rev. ed. New York: New American Library, 1950.

Krikorian, Y. H. (ed.). *Naturalism and the Human Spirit*. New York: Columbia University Press, 1944.

———. "Sources of Human Power," *Ararat*, 1960, 1:2, 32-34.

Lepley, R. (ed.). *The Language of Value*. New York: Columbia University Press, 1957.

Perry, R. B. *Realms of Value*. Cambridge: Harvard University Press, 1954.

Randall, J. H., Jr. "Dewey's Contribution to Scientific Humanism," *Humanist*, 1959, 19, 134-138.

7 Social Science and Values

ALFRED E. KUENZLI

A basic problem for human beings is that we have to *act*. We are decision-making organisms and there is no escape from having to direct our behavior along one path or another. We have to support, or *not* support, this cause or that cause. We have to take a stand on this side or that side of great social issues. Life catches us up and involves us in its processes, much as we might like, at times, to stand on the sidelines.

But there is a further problem for most of us in that we want to act *rightly*, ethically and constructively. And this leads to the question of how the person is to know whether his action is "right." In other terms, this is the problem of trying to find a reasonably solid base on which to build the good life. It is to this kind of concern that the following discussion is addressed.

One of the more fruitful approaches to the ethical problem is in terms of the concept of "uncertainty" which a number of psychologists, such as J. S. Bruner, have been employing in recent years so as to gain a more adequate understanding of human behavior. This principle recognizes that we are mere mortals, neither all-wise nor all-knowing, and that we are continually trying to make sense out of our lives.

It is not my purpose to discuss the many interesting ways in which people go about resolving the ambiguities underlying their existence. I only want to subscribe to the notion that action is *probabilistic*. To act is to take a kind of "moonlight gamble," based on *beliefs* at various degrees or levels of certainty.

This is to suggest that what we do is based on tacit assumptions or hypotheses or expectations. And I have no objection if someone wants to say that life is ultimately a matter of "faith." In fact, Hadley Cantril is probably right when he proposes, in naturalistic terms, that man needs to find a faith that will support his efforts to overcome the disillusionment and despair of today's world.

Critique of Religion

We all know that traditional religion has been the principal source of ethical authority in the life of the individual and that metaphysical pronouncements of priests have, for many persons, resolved some of the ambiguities underlying existence. Historically it has been the province of the clergy to discriminate the "black" acts from the "white," to tell us what kinds of behavior will get us into heaven or send us into hell. It is appropriate to note that the Church Federation of Chicago, in an effort to get religion taught in the public schools, has declared that "God is the ultimate sanction for moral and spiritual values in life."

But is this really the last word on ethics? Are there secular sources of moral and spiritual guidance that may be as satisfactory, or more so, than the supernatural sanctions of tradi-

tional religion? Is it possible, even, that the churches have
stood in the way of man's quest for ethical clarity and wisdom?

All sorts of horrible things have been done in the name
of "God," and the churches are notoriously divided as to
which are the sinful acts. Birth control, theatergoing, use of
alcoholic beverages or square dancing will send you to hell in
some of the churches but not in others. This is, I think, one of
the tragedies of traditional churches. They have not been
able to give persons very satisfactory moral guidance, especially on some of the larger questions of the day.

And these thoughts are remindful of the task that John
Dewey undertook in his Terry lectures—to emancipate us
from "religion" so that we can become "religious." One of his
indictments is that the churches have lagged behind in most of
the important social movements and that they have turned
their attention in social affairs mainly to moral *symptoms*—
to vices and abuses, like drunkenness, sale of intoxicants or divorce—rather than to the causes of war and the long list of
economic and political injustices.

A Normative Humanism

My contention is that a new source of ethical guidance
is emerging or *can* emerge, a source that is empirical in its
foundations and scientific in its method. I am speaking of so-
cial-psychological research. I am speaking of what Erich
Fromm, in his book *The Sane Society*, calls a "normative humanism." I have in mind the kind of *relative* certainty or ob-
jectivity that one gets after several pieces of research have

come to approximately the same conclusion. That is, a number of investigators have studied a problem and their results are comparable. This is not an *absolute* certainty that will be true for all time but there is enough certainty to give reasonable guidance in the world of here and now.

An example is the Supreme Court decision on desegregation. Most of us will recall that evidence from psychological research formed part of the basis out of which this major ethical judgment was made. The brief which was submitted to the Supreme Court contained an appendix—endorsed by thirty-two sociologists, psychologists and psychiatrists—entitled "The Effects of Segregation and the Consequences of Desegregation: A Social Science Statement."

Psychologist Kenneth B. Clark, who has studied the effects of discrimination on the personality development of minority-group children, points out that one of the ways in which the Supreme Court decision is momentous is that, for the first time in history, psychological evidence was admitted into a court of law as part of the basis on which a judgment of considerable ethical consequence could be made. He states: "In view of the fact that a systematic and empirical approach to the study of society is relatively new and the fact that legal arguments and decisions depend to such a large extent on precedent, the introduction of social science testimony was an extension of the legal frontiers."

Another example of the ethical guidance that can come from the social sciences is the thorough work that has been carried out in recent years in the field of child psychology. I believe we are now in a position to say, the Jesuits notwithstanding, that the "good" family is the "democratic" family. With Samuel Butler, I believe the evidence is leading most of us to reject the patriarchial family as not being conducive to human happiness and fulfillment. We are finding that participation by wives and children in family planning and decision-making tends to make for much greater harmony and solidarity than is the case where the father is "lord and master." And we hope that the incidence of delinquency, crime, divorce and mental illness will consequently be reduced.

The examples could be multiplied. There is the host of interesting questions which Sophia Fahs has raised about what kinds of religious teachings contribute to the healthy development and psychological well-being of children. Certainly the fears, anxieties, superstitions and unnecessary guilt feelings that have been implanted by many of the fundamentalist churches have not made the work of the clinical psychologist any easier.

It is to be granted, of course, that, for many persons, traditional religion has provided a basis for *enduring* life. But has it provided much of a basis for really *living* life? I am reminded of a worker, interviewed by Hadley Cantril in France, who said: "All I want is to enjoy myself in this life. For all I know it may be the only one I have. . . . What the workers want is a good standard of living and more opportunities for themselves and their kids."

Critique of Society

Ultimately the major question which the social sciences will need to answer is: what kinds of *structures*—in the family, the schools, the community and the sociopolitical system—will be most conducive to the full development of human personality? In answering this question, capitalism and other kinds of social organization will have to be brought under careful, dispassionate scrutiny.

At this early date in the emergence of the behavioral sciences, I shall not try to predict how contemporary capitalism will measure up to the criterion of human happiness and fulfillment. Certainly Fromm's critique in *The Sane Society* raises serious questions; nor does the Soviet system fare very well in a recent report from Harvard's Russian Research Center.

One of the most careful and provocative critiques of social structures that has been made so far is Floyd Hunter's study of "decision-makers" in Atlanta. A basic question which he raises at the conclusion of his book is whether the destiny of half a million people should be determined as fully as it is by about forty "men of power" who have control over social change within the community. This is, I submit, a deeply ethical question. It is a question that was brought to light by social research, not by divine revelation or mystical intuition. And it is likely that social research, rather than revelation or intuition, will give the most satisfactory guidance to the resolution of the problem.

As a matter of fact, what major social problem have we ever solved by way of extra-mundane sources? Certainly the gods have not done very well by us when it comes to preventing crime or neurosis or psychosis or war. The problem, as John Dewey put it, is that "men have never fully used the powers they possess to advance the good life, because they have waited upon some power external to themselves to do the work they are responsible for doing."

Facts and Values

Let me conclude with a brief discourse on the relationship of facts to values. Further consideration of this question,
at a more penetrating level, seems necessary to substantiate my
main point about an objective basis for ethics.

Traditionally we have distinguished between "facts" on
the one hand and "values" on the other. Typically we have
said that a fact is a statement about *what is* and a value is a statement about *what should be*. And we have tended to distinguish between "science" and "philosophy" on this basis also,
reserving the domain of values and ethics rather exclusively
for the philosopher.

I am aware, therefore, that any move in the direction of
merging the realms of "fact" and "value" will be perceived as
a threat by many philosophers as well as by most scientists. Let
it be said that my thesis is simply that values *can* be based on
facts, or that facts can be *coercive* on values, and in this sense
the relationship may be more intimate than we usually take it
to be.

Phenomenologically speaking, we have as our model an
individual with a belief system or what is sometimes called a
"cognitive structure." This structure contains the individual's
fairly established assumptions or knowledge about the world,
i.e., what he takes to be "facts" about his present surroundings.
The structure also contains a set of future-oriented predispositions and aspirations which we could call a person's "values,"
i.e., the kinds of things the individual views as worthwhile in
terms of his ongoing processes. Probably Eduard Spranger's

categories of the theoretical, economic, aesthetic, social, political and religious are useful at this point.

Seen in this way, there is at least a minimum relationship between facts and values in that both are components of an individual's cognitive structure. It is important to note that the facts existing in a person's world are always "quasi-facts," as Kurt Lewin put it, in that no individual can claim absolute certitude even though much of the time he may *feel* relatively certain about what he takes to be realities.

The point I would like to establish is that new data which the individual perceives about himself or his surroundings *can* be coercive on his predispositions and aspirations. Thus a person who discovers "the fact" that he has great artistic aptitude may come to increase his aesthetic "value." Or a person who learns that a number of dwellings in his community have only dirt floors and no indoor plumbing may develop a greater concern for his fellow men, i.e., he may come to increase what Spranger would call the "social" value.

To take an example from another culture and another age, I think that this kind of coercion of values by the data of experience is to be seen in the case of the Buddha. We recall that, according to the legend, the young prince went out from the palace and encountered an old man, then a sick man, then a dead man. These new "facts" about his surroundings, these new perceptions, were sufficiently coercive on his values that they led him to establish a new philosophical system—a set of aspirations and practices directly related to the data of his perception.

If these examples are sound, then it would seem that values could be based on empirical materials. And it would seem that two relatively rational individuals, exposed to the same data, would tend to hold the same values. I would like to propose, as a further illustration, that the tendency of social scientists to hold liberal values is by no means accidental.

A Greater Rationality

Of course this analysis is a simplification since we do not find many persons who are highly "rational" in a literal sense. The autistic aspects of our cognitive life have been well demonstrated through both psychoanalytic and perceptual research. We all perceive selectively, tending to deny or distort data that do not fit our assumptions about ourselves and our surroundings. Therefore our values are by no means completely open to the coercion of facts.

But it is entirely possible for us to become more aware of our selective and distorting tendencies. If we make an effort to do this, then those of us who would like to develop empirically oriented cognitive structures will be able to become, increasingly, the masters of ourselves and of our destiny.

My suggestions, then, are twofold: (a) we need to recognize the potential contribution of behavioral science research to the answering of large ethical questions; (b) we need to increase our capacities to utilize new data of experience that will be coercive on our values and hence on our ethics. In this way we can come to gain a reasonably objective basis for "right" action and we shall have a firm foundation on which to build the good life.

Bibliography

Bruner, J. S., *et al.* *A Study of Thinking.* New York: Wiley, 1956.

Butler, S. *The Way of All Flesh.* New York: Modern Library.

Cantril, H. *The "Why" of Man's Experience.* New York: Macmillan, 1950.

———. *The Politics of Despair.* New York: Basic Books, 1958.

Clark, K. B. "Desegregation: An Appraisal of the Evidence," *Journal of Social Issues,* 1953, 9, No. 4.

Dewey, J. *A Common Faith.* New Haven: Yale University Press, 1934.

Easton, D. "Shifting Images of Social Science and Values," *Antioch Review,* 1955, 15, 3-18.

Fahs, S. L. *Today's Children and Yesterday's Heritage.* Boston: Beacon Press, 1952.

Fromm, E. *The Sane Society.* New York: Rinehart, 1955.

Humphreys, C. *Buddhism.* Baltimore: Penguin Books, 1955.

Hunter, F. *Community Power Structure.* Chapel Hill: University of North Carolina Press, 1953.

Inkeles, A., *et al.* "Modal Personality and Adjustment to the Soviet Socio-Political System," *Human Relations,* 1958, 11, 3-22.

Kuenzli, A. E. "Where Society Suffocates Man," *New Republic,* 1956, 134:13, 19.

———. (ed.). *The Phenomenological Problem.* New York: Harper, 1959.

Part IV Freedom

8 Freedom for the Personality

The problem of freedom is one of the persistent perplexities that every generation encounters. As we look back and observe the gradual emergence of our present concepts and beliefs about freedom, it appears that freedom must always be relative to the climate of opinion, the sensibilities and the immediate occasions which have stimulated reflective thinking upon, and overt activities toward, the extension of freedom enjoyed by individuals.

It is especially appropriate today to stress this evolutionary and relative aspect of freedom because we are now passing through one of the more acute phases of the continuous process of transition that has characterized Western European culture. We need, therefore, the benefit of a long time-perspective with which to see our present situation in its due proportions and, above all, its scarcely revealed promise for the future. It is not intended, however, to essay an historical examination of the ideas of freedom, for which others are more competent, but rather to indicate a way of approach to the discussion of human freedom and to emphasize another dimension to that problem which has been largely neglected—the meaning of freedom for the personality.

We may be able to gain the needed perspective for such an enterprise by rehearsing somewhat briefly the conditions that generate the problem of freedom for man, especially for man within Western European culture.

Man and His Culture

We may therefore begin with a consideration of man and his culture, to use the term by which we designate the ideas, concepts and beliefs, patterns of conduct and feeling, the many different kinds of signs, symbols and rituals—together with the tools and techniques—that have served man as instruments for his uniquely human modes of life. It is only recently that we have become aware of culture as these historically developed patterns, which man has attempted to impose upon nature and himself in order that he might survive biologically and, more importantly, organize group life and regulate his conduct so that he could have what we call "social living."

As we have learned of other cultures and have discovered how the same geographic world of nature and the same basic activities and functions of man have been so variously conceived, patterned and ordered, we have become more keenly aware of our own culture and have slowly begun to realize that we can see, think, speak, act and feel only as our culture has given us the awareness, the concepts, the symbols, the patterns and the sanctions. Our efforts today to understand what culture does to and for the individual are still handicapped not only by this relative unawareness of culture but also by the ancient idea of society as some mysterious, cosmic organization operating through superhuman or supernatural forces to which man must obediently submit.

Moreover, we have the long-established, historical tradition—carrying the most venerable and awful sanctions—that our basic concepts and beliefs have a supernatural origin which therefore renders them *inviolable to inquiry* or critical examination. We might hazard the suggestion that the twentieth century, and perhaps the major portion of the twenty-first century, will witness prolonged conflicts over the exigent questions concerned with culture—whether it is supernatural or humanly derived, whether it is susceptible to modification, and by what criteria the coming reorganization of Western European culture shall be directed.

Pursuing our immediate inquiry, we may say that man gained freedom from the demands and limitations of a primarily biological existence by and through the development of his culture. Instead of being controlled by physiological functions which insistently drive all other species to pursue their fulfillment, man has learned to emancipate himself to a greater or lesser extent from the more exigent control of hunger, of eliminations and of the acute emotional reactions which —if left unregulated—would leave him at the mercy of functions and impulse.

Moreover, man has found through culture a way of enjoying a degree of freedom for his person and for his belongings by observing the inviolability of others—called the sanctity of the person—and of things—called private property. This inviolability of the person has been of special significance, because it has made possible man's freedom from the coercion of his own sex impulses and from exposure to unrestrained sex exploitation by others.

But culture has served not only as a way of managing man's own organic functions and impulses that would otherwise rule his existence with their imperious biological demands. Culture has also provided man with the patterns of conduct whereby he could manage to live in groups—respecting the inviolability of the person and the property of others, sharing in that division of labor which tools and techniques make necessary and, above all, finding in the use of group-accepted and group-sanctioned symbols, rituals and institutional practices—such as contract, barter, courtship and marriage, voting—the common modes of communication, negotiation and person-to-person relationships. This human organization and group living should be sharply distinguished from the animal aggregations and communities which arise, as in the insects, from highly specialized, organic structures and capacities—which not only provide for the differentiated activities necessary to an organization but likewise forever prevent any modification of that specialized form of community living.

This amazing service of culture to man is not limited, however, to his organic functioning or to his group organization. It goes further, in providing him with a way of conceiving and dealing with the world of nature that presents itself, precariously and problematically—offering the only resources for living, yet at the same time threatening man directly by its own order, regularity and complete disregard of values. Faced with such a world of nature, man has sought to allay his anxiety and to find both reassurance and the more concrete patterns and sanctions for his relations to that world through the basic ideas and concepts that he has created for his commerce with nature. Through these ideas, which have at once recog-

nized the enormity and seeming ruthlessness of nature but yet
have given man both the courage and the approach to wrest his
security from nature, we see how culture has enabled man to
come to terms with the universe—not by accepting and sub-
mitting, but by creating his own realities.

Culture is an imaginative creation—a deliberate attempt,
like the work of the artist, to give form, proportion, meaning,
significance and value to experience. It necessitates rearrange-
ment, suppression, selection and all the other discriminating
activities with which the artist works in order to give dimensions and proportions—thereby helping us to become aware,
not merely of the natural world surrounding us but, more importantly, of the aesthetic configurations which come from the
artistic imagination and sensitivity and, above all, from the
courage and daring to create something that is more meaningful than nature itself.

The Emergence of Personality

If the foregoing offers a valid basis for a discussion of human personality and conduct, we may point out some of its
major implications for the question of freedom for the personality.

The historic conception of human nature and conduct
has stressed man as a rational animal, as one who can and does
use "reason" as a guide to conduct—weighing situations and
alternatives and choosing among them in accordance with various criteria, among which that of self-interest has been predominantly recognized. This psychological theory of motivation and of conduct has received its fullest expression and elab-

oration in theology, in law and the various social theories where the autonomy of human conduct is assumed as a basis for ethics—the legal rules regulating the individual's rights, titles, obligations and interests—and as an explanation for the observed behavior of man in his economic, political and other social activities.

As we look back over the historic development of Western European cultures, as expressed in the different ethnic or nationalistic groupings that make up the shifting political units of Western Europe, it is evident that in different periods and in different countries there has been a continuous struggle among different groups within the populations over the limitations that might be imposed upon the individual's action, speech and belief. Our major preoccupation has been, therefore, with these overt aspects of individual activity and with the guarantees against restraint upon or interference with action, speech and belief. The underlying assumption has been that "rational man," given the opportunity and left unfettered by social restraints, can and will exercise his right to act, to speak and to believe in such ways as will bring him individually what is essential to human life and dignity and will insure a social life that will foster a rational human mode of existence.

To say that the foregoing represents the basic assumptions upon which the Western European societies have proceeded for many generations is not to offer any pronouncement but rather to indicate a way of interpreting our historical development and of revealing the preoccupations with which many of our present-day discussions of freedom are conducted. These statements will also serve as an effective background for a further discussion of freedom that contrasts sharply with this official, rationalistic conception.

If we recall the process of enculturation and socialization through which the child is made a participating member of his culture and of his society, it will be remembered that at every stage in this process adults are engaged in the systematic interference with, and redirection of, the basic biological or mammalian pattern of functional activity and the inculcation of the amazingly complicated beliefs and concepts and patterns of conduct and feeling with which the young individual is enabled to live in the common public world which his culture has selectively organized for the guidance of its members. The surrender of physiological autonomy by the young infant occurs when he accepts these interferences and, above all, the deprivations required by weaning, toilet training and the management of impulses and emotions.

Moreover, the basic social patterning of his conduct necessitates his learning to inhibit his impulsive behavior toward other persons and things so as to respect their inviolability and also his learning to perform the many prescribed actions deemed essential to his or her sex, class, rank, status and other social obligations. These deprivations and frustrations, these inhibitions and coercions—beginning at birth or shortly after —arouse anxiety which colors the idiomatic world which the child constructs from such experiences. If these early experiences make the child feel the world is *threatening and hostile,* he can only build his private world accordingly; if they are reassuring and comforting he can develop confidence in the world as *hospitable and benevolent* and can create his private world with those meanings.

What is of greatest significance is that these lessons in socialization create *persistent affective reactions* or feelings toward life which direct the child's subsequent experience and control his later learning. So long as we think of human conduct in terms of completely rational processes and volition, and recognize only the so-called conscious memory of what can be verbalized, it is difficult to realize how coercive these early experiences are and how these initial feelings toward life dominate the individual's whole life career. When we see human conduct as arising from *selective awareness*, the persistent affective set or expectation toward life, then we can better understand the dynamic process of human personality and conduct.

Just as we have learned in physics and chemistry, and now in biology, that the previous experience of any energy complex continues to operate in the present because the past experience is not out in some mysterious realm but is just this persistent modification of the energy complex that continues to operate in the present, so in the consideration of human conduct we are beginning to see that these early experiences of childhood—when the infant is just beginning to construct his private world and to organize those patterns of feeling that will be coercive over subsequent experience—continue to operate in every attempt the child makes to order events, to organize experience and to learn to regulate his conduct.

We may point out here how the traditional concept of man stands in the way of our accepting this viewpoint towards human conduct. But we shall see that, without a conception of the coercive role of early experience, human conduct remains inexplicable and continues to baffle every effort to achieve any measure of the social order we so desperately need.

If we recall, therefore, how these early experiences initiate a continuous process wherein the child meets every new situation with the expectation and the feeling engendered by his past experience, then we may see how not only this early physiological training but all the subsequent lessons in learning the inviolabilities—in accepting the socially required compulsions—are but a continuation of the same process of coercive and often distorting experience to which the child submits because he must, but which gives rise to a subjective realm of thoughts, beliefs and feelings. We need only pause to recall how our own personal lives are led in terms of this inner monologue and the constant interplay of feelings which, with adult years, we have learned to hide so adroitly behind the outer mask of adult conformity and seeming poise.

Personality and Freedom

Where these considerations lead is to a progressively clearer conception of the personality as this dynamic process of organizing experience so that every situation, person and event is fitted into the patterns which the official culture and the social requirements have prescribed—but always with that bias and distortion, that selective awareness and those peculiar feelings that our individual life experience has made the basic dimension of our private world. We spend our days preoccupied with the effort to *maintain* this private world, like the spider carefully repairing its web after each shock or invasion, never relaxing our vigilance in any personal encounter—which we assess either as reinforcing or threatening this inner, private world.

Caught in this private world, we can only rarely understand the subjective reality of another or fumblingly communicate. As Thomas Mann has so well expressed it in *Joseph in Egypt:*

"The world hath many centres, one for each created being, and about each one it lieth in its own circle. Thou standest
but half an ell from me, yet about thee lieth a universe whose
centre I am not but thou art."

Here it becomes appropriate to point out that whatever
opportunities the social life may afford for the individual to
think, believe and act are, of necessity, either *limited* or *extended* by this highly individualized and personalized acceptance and utilization of such opportunities. Again the historical
tradition of "rationality" serves to obscure what is so clearly
shown in all our conduct as we see individuals in little groups
accepting and rejecting what their society and their communal
life offer—always in terms of the very idiomatic patterns of
their special orientation. For each of these cultural and social
variations there is usually a well-articulated statement of justification—often expressed in the form of a vigorous polemic
against those whose patterns of life differ—and always with the
invocation of whatever sanctions are utilized by that group
from among the many available in its culture.

It has been the boast of the so-called democratic societies,
and it has been a special characteristic of Western European
culture, that between the recurrent periods of oppressive in-
tolerance there has been offered the widest range of variation
to individuals and to such subcultural groups. When heresy
hunting has been rife, Western European culture has been torn
by internal conflicts over these variant sects but there is still
discernible a long-term, secular trend toward the progressive
toleration of deviants.

When we consider, however, the *personality* aspects of
this situation, our perspective on this historical process shifts
rather sharply and our approach to the present-day perplexi-

ties and conflicts is seen in a new light. What we begin to realize is that however much a society may offer the possibility of individual variation and, more specifically, may guarantee what we call "freedom" of action, speech and belief, nevertheless each individual can *utilize* that freedom only as his personality organization will permit. Therefore we are called upon to see each individual as engaged in doing what he must; his life experience will permit him to be aware of only what his past has given him to know and to act only as that past requires. We are, to phrase it tautologically, what we are because we have been what we have been.

The Affective Distortions

Yet even this statement of how the individual is coerced by his past experience yields but a partial insight into human conduct and personality expression because more coercively than the patterning of action by past experience is the *pervasive distortion* of human conduct by those persistent, affective reactions that arise in childhood and continue to function throughout our life careers. As the individual has been reared in early childhood, so will his personality process and his affective reactions to life operate, and so will they continue to operate, scarcely modified by any process of "reason" or other control so long as the individual has no awareness of how these affective processes are operating in his personal life.

We can see how this takes place by looking at the concrete situations in our lives today. We are confronted with the pathetic picture of individuals who in their early childhood have been unnecessarily deprived, frustrated and coerced and so have built up a private world which is forever insecure and threatened; hence they must react with *resentment and hostility* to every experience. Within their own private world are continually operating these strong feelings of resentment and hostility, which may be expressed in overt reactions against people or may operate as a subtle distortion of everything they do—leading to constant sabotage and destruction, always within a range that protects them from retaliation or official punishment.

Again we see how the early childhood experiences of being socialized by those who exercised their authority brutally have created a persistent resentment toward all authority so that throughout the life of the person who has been humiliated in this manner there is a constant endeavor to thwart, if not to challenge, everyone in positions of authority or control. Again, all through the early experiences of childhood, the young child, who is striving to meet the demands made upon him, is under constant tension which is crystallized into *a persistent anxiety about his own competence and functional adequacy* so that he goes through life obsessed by anxieties that may become focused upon the most extraordinarily irrelevant activities and events, or upon his own bodily functions. He acts as one who is compulsively directed to perform actions that are either absurd or obstructive to the common life or are disturbing to his physiological processes.

Perhaps the most frequent of all these personality distortions are the persistent feelings of hostility that become channeled into a constant endeavor to "get even," to *prove* that one is not as worthless or as wicked as one has been made to believe or to *retaliate* for all the humiliations and brutalities of the past. Then too there are the individuals who, in spontaneous exercise of those activities common to all young mammals, have transgressed the moral code of their elders and have been overwhelmed with reproach and punishment that have established *persistent feelings of guilt*, for the atonement of which they spend their adult lives.

Thus we might go on enumerating many different forms of persistent, affective reactions that color and distort the personality, driving the individual to engage in the most astonishing varieties of activities that bring little or no satisfaction of basic human needs and aspirations but nevertheless are exhibited by the individual because this coercive past experience forces him to their performance. If the recital of these reactions seems to be predominantly unwholesome, destructive and, to use a term that has become progressively meaningless, "abnormal," it is not to signify that human nature is, in accordance with the theological tradition, innately wicked, sinful, fallen from grace, antisocial and destructive. Nor is it to ignore or deny the acute hunger of every individual to be loved and to receive affection, to be accepted and cherished as a person of some worth and consequence to others.

The insistence on these distorted and destructive affective reactions is only a recognition of their greater frequency—eloquent testimony of what Western European culture does to and for the personality of the growing child who is terrorized, humiliated and often brutalized while being socialized. There are other cultures in which children are not terrorized, humiliated and brutalized—are not filled with persistent feelings of anxiety and guilt, of hostility and resentment—because the process of acculturation and socialization is conducted with affection, tenderness and benevolent patience which recognizes that the young human mammal can be brought within the range of social requirements only through *a warm, cherishing nurture*. And it is to be observed that in those cultures where the socialization of the child is conducted in this manner the social life is not disrupted by the aggressive, destructive, exploitive individuals from whom Western European culture has suffered for so many centuries.

In every culture the individual is of necessity "cribbed, cabinned and confined" within the limitations of what his culture tells him to see, to believe, to do and to feel—the limitations which man can never escape because he can live only in a cultural world which he himself creates and imposes upon himself. But, within the range of these limitations, the individuals who have been benevolently reared and wisely and patiently socialized may and apparently do possess that freedom which only the undistorted personality can enjoy.

It is becoming evident that every culture fosters a dominant character structure or socially preferred pattern of life and of expression in and through which the individual expends his energies and finds some release for his own anxieties and guilt. Likewise each culture creates the peculiar distortions of personality which the group-sanctioned methods of socialization produce in the child. The bearers of this official character structure and of these personality distortions are the active agents in the social, economic, political and other activities of the group. We may therefore regard the social conflicts and disorders as essentially symptoms of the cultural traditions of the group and of the character structure and personality expressions of its members.

The Problem of Social Order

This discussion has led us rather far from the present-day preoccupation with forms of government, laws and the innumerable complications of contending groups and individuals. As we have examined the process of acculturation and of socialization and attempted to trace the emergence of personality as itself a dynamic process of organizing experience and of reacting affectively to life, these contemporary issues have become progressively attenuated from their positions as major foci of interest and have become symptoms of the basic, underlying conflicts of Western European culture and of the unhappy, distorted and perverted personalities it fosters. We begin, then, to realize how our need for social order and our aspirations toward the enduring human values are continually frustrated and destroyed by these distorted personalities who are driven by their private worlds to seek release for their intolerable feelings and warped beliefs.

So long as we were at the mercy of supposed coercive social organizations—viewed as a part of a cosmos operating through mysterious social forces above and beyond man's reach or control—and so long as we viewed our culture as having been given us from supernatural sources and therefore to be accepted without critical inquiry or questioning, and so long as we conceived of human nature as innately predetermined according to theological tradition, just so long did the fate of man appear tragically determined. In the face of these cosmic immensities and these unchangeable verities, what could man do but cherish the wisdom of the past that taught him how best to protect himself in a world of that construction? Even though modern science has banished many of the larger terrors and superstitions which have for so many ages dominated man's thinking and beliefs, it has still left him at the mercy of these cultural and social and psychological beliefs that have so completely governed his attempts at ordering group life and individual expression.

Today we are faced with the prospect that is so extraordinary in all its implications that we have scarcely the courage to examine them. We now begin to see that culture is an historical creation of *man himself*—not a supernatural structure imposed on man but rather the product of his own efforts to order events, organize group life and regulate conduct in accordance with the sensibilities and the aspirations which he himself has created for the guidance of his own life. Social life, instead of being a cosmic organization operating by inexorable laws and forces, likewise is being revealed as an historical creation, arising from man's efforts to meet the persistent tasks of life to which each generation addresses itself in terms of the ideas, conceptions, beliefs, patterns of conduct and—above all —the sensibilities and feelings that are operating in his life.

Finally, we are beginning to see that the human personality emerges as the individual's way of life—his peculiar, idiomatic way of ordering events, organizing experience and reacting affectively to situations and people as a direct consequence of how he has been enculturated and socialized. Thus the conception of human freedom becomes not mainly an issue of overt action, speech and expressed beliefs, but rather freedom from the *personality distortions* and the *destructive affects* which make this overt freedom an ironic tragedy—since the individual may be compelled to use those possibilities not only for destruction of others but for his own frustration and defeat. The acute irony of this situation is in the incalculable damage inflicted upon human life by these unhappy personalities whose warped, twisted lives are derived from their childhood when love, affection, patience and understanding of human needs would have made different personalities.

So long as we are coerced by these persistent affective reactions of anxiety, guilt, shame and hostility, we do not enjoy freedom—no matter how much we are unrestrained by external limitations upon our actions, speech and belief. We are not only dominated by these feelings which we rarely recognize or acknowledge but we are at the mercy of those who, by playing upon these feelings, can use and exploit us as they wish. We can see this more clearly in the dictator states, but also in the democracies where we are becoming aware of how the citizens are skillfully manipulated by political and other leaders who cynically evoke these repressed feelings in order to control voting behavior. Indeed political strategy is based upon the solid expectation that the individual will always sacrifice or forego his own advantage, and even his basic requirements, in order to express his warped personality distortions and to release his otherwise repressed feelings.

In the light of these considerations and insights we may begin to reformulate the problem of freedom as more than freedom to act, speak and believe, as we recognize the imperative necessity of freedom for the personality from these distortions and destructive affects which so coercively dominate the individual's life—compelling him to utilize his freedom of action, speech and belief so largely for self-defeating and socially destructive expressions.

We can and must undertake this reformulation and accept the new tasks it sets because we are, somewhat reluctantly, realizing that the democratic aspirations cannot be realized nor be adequately expressed in and by voting and representative government. Democracy, or the democratic faith, is being reformulated today in terms of the value and integrity of the individual, not as a tool or means, but as an end or goal for whose conservation and fulfillment social life must be reoriented. Indeed, democracy reveals its essential meaning only as we see it as a continuous assay of our culture and of our society in terms of their *human consequences*—of what they do to and for human life and personality.

Thus freedom for the personality may be viewed as the crucial issue of a democratic society, for which we must seek to develop individuals who can accept all the inhibitions and requirements necessary to group life—without these distortions and coercive, affective reactions. Only then will we discover what human freedom means and how to achieve the enduring human values we have for so long vainly sought.

Bibliography

Childe, V. G. *Man Makes Himself.* New York: New American Library, 1952.

Frank, L. K. "The Fundamental Needs of the Child," *Mental Hygiene*, 1938, 22, 353-379.

———. *Society As the Patient.* New Brunswick: Rutgers University Press, 1949.

———. "Potentialities of Human Nature," *Humanist*, 1951, 11, 63-70.

———. *Nature and Human Nature.* New Brunswick: Rutgers University Press, 1951.

Huxley, J. *Man Stands Alone.* New York: Harper, 1941.

Lee, D. *Freedom and Culture.* New York: Prentice-Hall, 1959.

Muller, H. J. *The Uses of the Past*. New York: Oxford University Press, 1957.

Redfield, R. *The Primitive World and Its Transformations*. Ithaca: Cornell University Press, 1953.

——. *The Little Community*. Chicago: University of Chicago Press, 1955.

9   Tomorrow's Children

BROCK CHISHOLM

Only recently is it becoming generally recognized that the role of the parent in relation to the upbringing of a child is perhaps the most important thing that happens in our culture. Also, it is being recognized that much has been learned about the process of development during the first five or six years of life. Psychologists, cultural anthropologists, sociologists and psychiatrists have learned quite a bit about how children develop from birth toward maturity. But very little of that knowledge is yet implemented. In a few great centers of population, a few up-to-date people—aware of the world's present situation, aware of all the attempts to learn, to explore, to experiment—are thinking about these problems and are trying to straighten them out and to present us with a reasonably true picture for our consideration.

To be sure, the knowledge we have in the fields of human relations and child development is still crude; it is far from perfected. But it is usable and is far more worthy of our confidence than are the "certainties" that were inculcated in us in our childhood—"certainties" conditioned by the accident of birth and heredity. Whatever the limitations of present knowledge, it is a great improvement over the old habit of copying

the patterns of our ancestors simply because they were the patterns of our ancestors.

It should be obvious, then, that our responsibility now is
to help our children learn things and learn in ways that were
not available to us when we were children. If they are going to
make the kind of world in which security can be found, they
will have to develop free of many limitations that still bind us.

The Liberation of Beliefs

Many people who themselves have developed away from
the "certainties"—religious and other—inculcated in them in
their childhood, who no longer believe what they were taught
when they were children, send their children back, by their
own teaching or by that of others, to learn things in terms
which they themselves have discarded.

This is very queer but it happens frequently. Such people differentiate between good and true. Some attitude, some
belief, may no longer be considered "true" by the parents but
they earnestly think that their child should believe it because
it is "good." This contortion that many parents go through
discounts entirely all the development of any one generation.
It forces each generation to start all over again and to have to
go through the same long, slow, painful process of fighting
for liberation from binding "certainties" that were imposed
in childhood. If children are lucky, before they die they may
get to the same level their parents reached—but they won't
get much farther.

This is unfair to children. Surely one's children should
be given the advantages of one's own development. Surely

they should not be tied hand and foot all over again as their parents were tied to the absolutes of the past generation. Millions of children in the world are now being tied to the certainties of ten and twenty and thirty generations ago by this mechanism wherein each generation refuses to let its children continue from the point it itself reached.

By advocating that we should free our children of the "certainties" of their ancestors, I do not mean that we should abolish religion or religious teaching. One cannot deny that, throughout human history, religion has been a tremendously important part of people's lives. It has represented, episodically at least, an attempt *to understand*—a striving to find this harmonious living about which we try to talk scientifically.

I am not suggesting that no one needs religion or that we should become antireligious and get rid of it. Not only do many people need some kind of religion, they need different kinds of religion. They need different beliefs, and if they have that need, they should be free to seek whatever it is that they need.

What I am suggesting is that they should not be tied to the system of beliefs to which their parents happen to adhere, beliefs often acquired through the accident of birth into a particular family at a particular time in a particular place. Surely the time has come when the human race should learn to take charge of its own destiny and no longer submit itself to the mercy of these accidents.

It is the teaching of unchangeable attitudes that makes trouble. The problem is not created nearly so much by the content of an orthodoxy as by the fact of an orthodoxy. It is not the teaching of an attitude—however it is taught—that is damaging nearly so much as the teaching that it is *fixed and final* and that one is forbidden to think about it. This is damaging because children very early in their lives get the idea they should stop their thinking every time they run into anything uncomfortable or dangerous or threatening.

Children need to make their peace with religion—everybody does in some way—but it is hard to justify the parents who will prescribe one particular religion for their children in a way that can make them feel guilty, ashamed and subject to a variety of neurotic difficulties if they dare to change their minds about it.

I believe that every child should be taught in his early years the facts of religion, the tremendous importance that religion has had in the lives of most of the people of the world; that he should be helped to understand what religion has done, what it has done *for* people and what it has done *to* them; how it has been used effectively and satisfactorily under some circumstances and disastrously under others.

The principles of all the great religions, the ethical attitudes, are much the same—giving or taking a little on account of the particular culture in which a particular religion developed—but the expression of them is the expression that is typical of the culture and it can not be anything else. The child should be taught this.

One of the commonly shared religious codes is the Ten Commandments. As in many other schemes of ethics, there is very much truth and wisdom in them—but some of them, I think, are not as wise as others, shall we say? For instance, the injunction to honor thy father and mother that thy days may be long in the land was perfectly satisfactory in the kind of system in which it was said; that is, if you didn't honor your father and mother, they were entitled to do you in—it was that kind of society.

But honoring fathers and mothers now does not necessarily lengthen one's days at all. I think it is much more satisfactory to see mothers and fathers clearly—and they will be honored if they are honorable, they will be respected if they merit respect, they will be loved if they are lovable. But commanding children to do that sort of thing is totally futile. It doesn't have any useful effect or value.

In fact, I do not believe the imposing of any commandments on children is effective. I believe that they need an object lesson before them, a picture of what man-and-woman behavior is like at its best—as seen in their fathers and mothers —and then they will grow into that picture more satisfactorily than will children who have commandments imposed upon them.

There are such things, of course, as matters of faith. This, I believe, the child needs to be told perfectly clearly— that something is a matter of faith with the parent. And then it should be explained why the parent believes in or has this particular faith. If it is the accident of his birth, the child should know it. If the parent has been convinced by someone's arguments, that too needs to be told to the child. But the important thing to remember is that just because the parent has adopted a faith, it is not necessarily at all the best faith for a child—or for a child when he grows up. That should be for him to decide, not the parent or anybody else.

Truthfulness in Teaching

Because the childhood of every person remains part of him all his life, it surely is reasonable to suggest that we should never teach anything to children that is not literally true, because children have very literal minds. We must realize that childhood and adulthood are continuous. No person is one year old and then stops being one year old and becomes two years old. No person is five years old and stops being five years old and is ten years old, or stops being ten years old and is twenty or thirty or forty years old.

Every person is the accumulated sum of his whole experience. There is a one-year-old in every grown-up extant, still there, with the attitudes the one-year-old child had. Every person extends from his infancy to his latest development, but he doesn't stop being one thing when he takes on something else. He adds his experience to his accumulated total; thus there is a part of every person that has the necessities of the infant, the necessities of the child also, the necessities of the juvenile, the young adult, and eventually added to it the necessities of the old person. Each part of this extended personality needs its particular types of satisfaction.

This concept is important. Many people feel that it doesn't matter very much what you teach a two-year-old child because he is going to stop being a two-year-old child and after a while will be a five-year-old child, which is a different thing. It isn't. The two-year-old child is still the basis, the foundation, for the five-year-old child, and the five-year-old child is the first or second or fifth story of the building that will be the adult later on. If the five-year-old child is broken up in pieces, if he has conflicts within his personality, if parts of himself are at war with other parts of himself, it will be extremely difficult for him to act as a sound foundation for the grown-up person that he will later become. If continual building goes on, as it does in every intelligent person, on the foundation of childhood experience, by the time he has added thirty or forty or fifty stories, as it were, the stability of the early stories becomes tremendously important. It will determine whether the upper levels of his structure will stand or not, because the early stories are still part of the personality— indeed they are the very foundation of every personality.

This, I think, we have not learned sufficiently. When we think about it, we all know that it is true and yet we feel that we have a license to misinform children without any feeling of irresponsibility—to tell them weird things, even to teach them things or have other people teach them things that we don't believe ourselves.

This, of course, is unfair not only to the individual child but also socially—unfair to the human race—because the human race cannot afford to have good material spoiled, good material which might contribute to its eventual security.

These are responsibilities that lie firmly on parents. Nobody else can take their place. Later on, teachers may help but a teacher may spend all his time and effort in trying to repair some of the damage done by parents without doing any really constructive thing, just repairing damage. If that is necessary—and it may take years to repair the damage, if it can ever be done at all—much time is wasted, and the child will probably not be able to develop to anywhere near the degree of maturity that he should have been able to reach if his parents hadn't crippled him when he was very young.

Most of our children are exposed to lies regularly. Parents generally have two entirely separate standards of truth—one for children and one for everybody else. Of course there are parents who simply lie to everybody, but even for those who consider themselves "honest," lying to children seems to be entirely outside the moral code.

I remember being tremendously impressed with this phenomenon years ago when I was doing observation work in a child-development clinic. It always bothered me a little, because we sat behind windows which could be seen through only one way. Thus these children were rather defenseless because they didn't know there were any grown-ups about. They weren't under pressure to behave in ways that would preserve the illusions of their parents or other adults, and so they behaved naturally.

I saw two little boys, one of whom was in trouble. He would be about four, I suppose, and an older boy—perhaps six or a little more—was persecuting him, making him very unhappy. The smaller boy, tears in his eyes but not quite crying, was saying, "It does so! It does so!" The bigger boy, being very superior, was saying, "It does not! Don't be silly. It does not!" This exchange continued for a few minutes and then the little boy put his hands over his ears and said, "I won't listen to you! It does so!"

The bigger boy pulled the smaller one's hands away from his ears and hooted, "The sun does not go to bed at night. How could it go to bed? There's no bed in the sky, is there, dopey?"

The smaller child broke down and, with tears running down his face, sobbed, "It does so go to bed at night! My daddy told me!"

And at that moment he realized his father had lied to him; it was a deep tragedy, one from which he probably will not recover completely.

I don't suppose that his father even considered the question of whether he was lying to his son or not, but he was. He was misinforming the child as to the facts of life and a child of four is very busy building a picture of his universe, building a picture of the reality in which he is going to have to learn to live. If his father, at that stage, tells him that the sun goes to bed at night, imagine how it distorts his picture of the world about him.

Now I suppose that a fabrication about the sun going to bed at night seems like a simple and harmless lie. But to the intelligent child it leads inevitably to the question "Who tucks him in?" because, when you go to bed at that age, somebody boosts you up and tucks you in, kisses you and opens the window, turns out the light. This is "going to bed" and there is no other way of going to bed from a child's point of view. He is only seeking honest information when he asks this question.

What is he to be told? That the moon tucks in the sun before she comes up? Is this to become the basis of the reality that is being formed for this child at four years of age? Does any of us suppose that this child has a very good chance of ever being able to function as a world citizen with that amount of distortion at four years old? Cracks in his foundation, things out of place, things that he can't depend on? But the most important thing is that he can't depend on his father, and if he can't depend on his father to tell the truth, how can he depend on anybody?

Mistrust is the lesson that very many children learn from the habitual lies of their parents about quite casual things that don't seem important to parents but are the very stones and bricks on which a child's life and relationship to reality are being built. There is no good whatever in our telling our children that they should grow up to be able to "live harmoniously in a changing total environment" if, in their early childhood, we distort the reality of the environment, if we make it nonsense to them, if we make it a place where cause and effect mean nothing—a place where thinking only gets them into the unfortunate position of not being able to trust anybody, or even their own power of observation and thinking.

This has been done to most of us when we were children, with the best of intentions, our parents not knowing any better. It was done to our parents, and to their parents, and most of the people in the world are still doing the same sort of thing to their children.

Please do not suppose that when I say we should always tell the truth to children I mean to suggest that the fairy tale should be rooted out. The fairy tale, the myth, the Santa Claus, all these things are charming and even valuable—*as myths*. What I do mean is that every child should know, before he has a fairy story read or told to him, that it isn't true. If he doesn't know that, the parent is not helping him to get in touch with reality.

When a child is very small, fantasy and reality are not distinct. One of the major problems that a child has to solve during his development is how to sort out fantasy and reality, so that he knows when he is dealing with real things and when he is dealing with fantasy. This is an extremely important achievement—the ability to know with certainty what is fantasy and what is reality. It forms the basis for a sound imagination—a most desirable quality—but if the lines are not clearly drawn, if the parents do not help the child to distinguish between fantasy and reality, the child may—as many people do—go on through his life without ever clearly grasping what the difference is. He will grow up without thinking in terms of cause and effect: "Who knows? A fairy may come along and fix everything up so that I need not suffer the uncomfortable results of what I did." It is easy to see that such thinking is conducive to irresponsible behavior later on.

But let us not do away with fairies and Santa Claus. Let us play them as games. Children are capable of imagining harmlessly as long as they know they are imagining. They can imagine little playmates of all kinds; they can imagine all sorts of animals, all kinds of people without any damage whatever—as long as that fantasy isn't supported seriously by grown-ups.

The Importance of Love

We know more now than we used to about the kinds of things that handicap children's development, and we know what the needs of children are. If a small child is given sufficient food and sufficient shelter, sufficient water or moisture to stay alive, the next requirement is *love*—close, warm, physical-contact love.

The time has gone when psychologists and psychiatrists

blush when they use the word "love." Love has now become
a scientific term (which makes it respectable) and is now recognized as a good thing. Indeed, it is now considered indispensable—or nearly so—in early childhood for effective emotional development toward maturity.

In this area, in our wonderfully advanced North America, oddly enough, we are behind certain other cultures when
it comes to loving our babies. We have acquired some rather
dreadful habits—all in the name of Hygiene.

I am reminded of the time, some years ago, when I was
in Pakistan, and was being guided through a very large general hospital. As we were going along a corridor, which was a
sort of balcony on the side of the building, we passed the
screened door to a ward. Suddenly someone pointed out to
me, with great enthusiasm, something away off on the horizon
in the opposite direction. Now, to any old Army inspecting
officer, the situation was perfectly clear; there was something
nearby they didn't want me to see. Therefore I was quite sure
that whatever was hidden behind this screened door I should
see. If you see only what people want you to see you will
never find out anything.

So I insisted—at some risk of offense—on seeing this
ward. When I insisted, my guides began apologizing, saying
that I wouldn't really like to see it at all; it was of a very old
pattern; they were ashamed of it; they hoped to get it
changed; they hoped that the World Health Organization
might help them get the money to adopt modern and new patterns for this particular ward, because it was very bad indeed.

However, I still insisted that even as an antiquity I
would like to see it. I went in to see this ward, with the reluc-
tant accompaniment of the train of people with me, and I saw

the best maternity ward I have ever seen in any country—far better than any I have ever seen in North America. Here was a big maternity ward with beds down both sides. The footposts of each bed were extended up about three feet or so, and slung between the foot posts was a cradle. The baby was in the cradle, and I noticed as I looked down the ward that one squeak out of the baby and up would come the mother's foot, and with her toe she would rock the cradle. On the second squeak, which showed that the baby was really awake, she would reach into the cradle and take the baby into her arms, where a baby is supposed to be most of the time.

They wanted to get rid of that perfectly beautiful arrangement, to put their babies under glass the way we do, and to keep them in inspection wards where they can be seen at a distance by their loving fathers whenever they visit, and be taken to their mother if she is good and does as the nurse tells her! They wanted to do all that because we Westerners had given them the impression that all our methods are superior to theirs.

Those babies, if they develop an infection, recover from it twice as fast as ours do. These people are not producing little neurotic babies of one month old the way we are. Their babies do not feel themselves out in the cold world, do not feel that nobody loves them from the moment they are born, as many of ours do. Mothers in that part of the world regard as perfectly savage some of the customs they have heard about in North America where mothers actually take their babies to hospitals, leave them there, and go home. No mother in Southeast Asia would do such a thing. She would fight everybody in the hospital before she would leave her baby there and go home without it. And she is right, demonstrably right.

Whenever a baby comes to a hospital in that part of the world, the mother accompanies it, and does everything for the baby that does not require the services of a trained nurse or of a physician. The baby feels at home all the time, and recovers from operation or disease much faster than our babies do, and does not suffer from any neurotic disabilities as the result of illness, as ours do.

I am not suggesting that we copy all of the patterns of these other countries. We need to be discriminating about other people's customs as well as our own, but we can learn a great deal about human relations, about the upbringing of children, from other people. Whenever we become humble enough to learn with discrimination from others' experiments in living, we shall begin to progress more steadily than we are now. Unfortunately, we tend to regard our own living patterns as *fixed and final* and of universal value and so we naturally think everyone should copy us. This is just not true.

I have been discussing the small child's need for love as a primary condition of his effective development. Any threat to love, any risk of loss of love, is for a child a nightmare—a threatening barrier between him and his continuing exploration of life. Yet very many children run into the threat of loss of love very early in life, sometimes even within the first year. Whenever a child behaves in ways that are not acceptable to the ideas, attitudes and moral codes of his parents (particularly of his mother), he risks running into active disapproval. This is interpreted by the child as a threat of loss of love.

The very young child is not concerned at all with the local behavior customs of the natives; he is born not knowing anything about them. One can call him uncivilized, "born in sin" or just not grown up; they are all the same thing. He is a

"natural," born the way he is born. And, furthermore, there
are no laws anywhere saying what a child one year old should
be like; he is not in any danger whatever of coming into conflict with the laws of the land and being punished for it. All
he is in danger of is running into the certainties or rigidities
of his parents, but there is plenty of danger in that for most
children.

Most parents have rather unbending ideas about what a
small child should be like, how he should behave, what he
should and should not do—even about when he should do it
and when he should not. Most parents will not admit that
these are really only matters of convenience for themselves or
for the local customs of the natives, and that they have no real
universal validity whatever. When a child first begins to explore his environment—the world as he sees and feels it—he
doesn't know any rules. He has no taboos. He reaches out in
all directions to find out what it's like. He tries to ingest
everything because this is the primitive method of getting acquainted, but he finds that some things can be ingested to his
advantage and some things cannot. He learns to accept and to
reject, and his developing morality is based simply on what is
pleasant and what is found to be unpleasant.

But even today, when very small children behave in various natural ways, parents disapprove violently. The form of
behavior that gets almost certain disapproval lies in the sexual
area. That is, a one- or two-year-old child, exploring his total
environment, finds—among everything else in his reality—
his own genital area, and it still happens (though I hope and
believe not as frequently as it used to) that his mother has extremely rigid ideas about genital areas and expresses disap-

proval very emphatically when the child is caught engaging in such exploration.

The child should be exploring his total environment at that stage and there should be no taboos placed upon such exploration. This is generally acceptable, but apparently many mothers haven't been told about it or, if they have, they can't quite believe it because of the way they have been brought up themselves. Very many children meet violence for the first time in their lives from their mother at this stage of their development. It is still common for mothers to slap a child's hand and say to him, "Dirty! Dirty! If you do that, Mother won't love you any more."

This is a very damaging experience. The part of the child's physical equipment which is associated with basic intersexual relationship has been made dirty and its existence associated with loss of love rather than with the expression of love. This is very disturbing to the whole development of the child's relationship to the opposite sex.

As he grows older, the child is afraid to find out about sexual facts of life because this would associate his mother and his father with the badness and dirtiness that have been imposed on him as belonging to sexual equipment. To the young child, of course, genital organs are not sexual at all, only excretory; but large areas of human behavior will have been spoiled by this early disapproval, by these attitudes imposed on a small child before his intelligence, his experience and his freedom to think independently are sufficient for him to be able to defend himself against that type of misdirection.

This is just one example of how the intelligent child, then, at a very early age, is convinced of his sin. He is loaded

with a burden of guilt, fear and anxiety. Because the very
small child, busily trying to find out everything about the
total environment in which he is going to have to live, eager
to explore, to know, to experiment, and enjoying very much
all his urges, all the things he wants to do—the use of eyes,
nose, ears, hands, fingers, feet and legs—because this child
does not naturally subscribe to Mother's rules (that is, in terms
of the time at which he should do things, the place where he
should do them, or how he should do them—or if he should do
them at all), because he runs into the threat "If you do this or
don't do that, Mother won't love you any more," because he
feels that what he is doing is perfectly natural to him, he
reaches the conclusion that he is *just naturally bad*. And bad,
of course, means unlovable. Mother said so. And because he
dare not risk the loss of love, he learns very early in life that he
must go about pretending that he isn't bad, but pretending
that he is good, so that he will continue to be loved.

This is a very difficult position for a child to be in because he can never act freely any more. He must watch all the
time to see what he should do, what he is supposed to do. He
knows what he naturally would do, but this has been called
bad. He can hope only to learn from good people what they
expect of him.

His mother, by definition, is "good" in the child's eyes
because she is what good is. She decides what is good and
what is bad and is the primary authority on goodness and
badness. Even God is only brought in to support the mother.
He doesn't originate anything; the mother originates it. Two
different mothers on opposite sides of the street may have
quite different ideas of good and bad but God is made to support both of them, one just as firmly as the other.

The old saying that "Mother knows best" was regarded, and still is, in many places, as practically sacred. Few children have the temerity to ask how she knows, who told her, where she studied, what is her authority, whenever she says, "Mother knows best." Most children do not have that degree of freedom with their parents. They would be beaten down if they tried—not necessarily physically, but in one way or another. But Mother continues to make the rules.

Very many children, when these things happen to them, become shy, afraid to face new circumstances, afraid to meet new people, afraid of the dark, afraid of all kinds of things—irrationally afraid because they don't know how to cope with new circumstances at all. They have no confidence in natural behavior because they have learned that natural behavior is bad and disapproved of by good people. In unknown circumstances or new situations the child is afraid to act at all for fear he will be "found out" as bad and be discarded—unloved and unaccepted.

Thus the groundwork is laid, to a certain extent, for the beginning of the well-known "inferiority complex," which those of us who have become civilized forcibly in childhood must inevitably suffer from to one degree or another. The degree will depend on *the amount of fear* used to train us and on *how early* we were beaten into conformity with the local customs of the natives, as understood by our parents.

Of course, no parents deliberately do these things to their children. They do not coolly decide to hurt their children. They do not set out to impose an inferiority complex on a defenseless child. They are merely following the way they themselves were brought up, and they believe that this is the good way because it was imposed on them in childhood.

But it cannot be overemphasized that basic security comes from being loved or, more importantly, *from feeling loved when one is very small.* There is nothing new in this concept. Indeed, implied in all the world's great religions there has been the suggestion or the command that people should love each other, should "Love thy neighbor as thyself." The catch, of course, comes in the last bit, "as thyself." Most of us who were brought up to be moral children, "good children," a credit to our parents (according to the local customs of the natives) before we were four or five or six years old, *are incapable of loving ourselves* because we were convinced in early childhood that we were not naturally lovable. We could only appear to be lovable by pretending to be something other than what we were. And if we cannot love ourselves in a healthy way, then it is not possible for us to really love *anyone else* because we project our own hatred of ourselves onto other people.

The Necessary Learnings

We have been talking about what not to do to children —how not to bind them to the "certainties" of the past, how not to deceive them with so-called harmless lies, how not to stunt their emotional development with the cruelest threat of all—that of the loss of love. But our responsibilities lie much deeper than a negative or even a passive level. There are certain positive things that we can and *must* do for our children; there are certain positive things that we can and must teach them.

Our children need to learn, early in life, values that go away beyond the advantage of the group, the father, the mother, the family and the local natives. They can be introduced and should be introduced to *world values* long before they go to school, and children are capable of recognizing the existence and importance of such values if their parents show that knowledge and that feeling themselves.

We do know what teachers need in children who come to school for the first time, that is, well-educated and intelligent teachers who are free to think for themselves. They want children who have some points of view, some knowledges, freedoms to think—children who are not nailed to the mast of an absolute belief but who are capable of considering all peoples' attitudes and of finding what is useful in them and discarding what is not, on the initiative of their own intelligence and not because some of their ancestors said or wrote this or that—even if it was written down in a Constitution. Children need a sense of identity with the whole human race.

These are the kinds of attitudes that are needed when children come to school. The responsibility is overwhelmingly that of the parents, who should be able to introduce their children to certain facts, to orient them reasonably effectively in relation to *time*, so that they do not think and feel only in the present but feel themselves part of the long process of development—not just local time, not just since the birth of "myself" or "my father" or "my grandfather" but national time, human racial time, geological time, astronomical time. These concepts are well within the scope of a small child before he goes to school—not in detail, not in measurements or anything like that, but in knowledge that these things exist and are a part of human experience and are the context in which man is or is not going to survive. Particularly schools need children who are already *reaching forward into time*, ahead of themselves.

If parents spend all their money on payments for things they can't afford, so that they never have any money and are always being pressed or pushed and just living for the moment, their children are not going to get proper appreciation of future time. A child by the time he goes to school should, if his parents present an example, be able to save up whatever he needs for at least a week or a month ahead to get something more valuable than he could get with what he has now.

Nowadays and in our present culture, by the time a boy or girl is in his early twenties or even his middle teens, he needs to be able to function about ten years ahead so that he will be able to project ahead of himself a picture of the kind of person he proposes to be after ten years or so of education and training. Otherwise he will not plan his life; he will continue to be the creature of accident in this field as well as in many other fields.

In other areas as well, such as his relation to *place*, a child should have learned by the time he goes to school to feel at home anywhere in space. Of course, I do not mean this literally, but he should know of the existence of space and be aware of his relationship to it.

This task is much easier since the comic strips and television have "gone for" the space concept. To be sure it is somewhat distorted, but it's much better than not having any idea at all. It is very much better than the concept that many children used to get from their parents that there wasn't any place that mattered outside of the local community. It is rare to find a benefit from the comics but this, I think, is one: that children are escaping from their locality. It may be into fantasy, but still it is an enlargement of experience beyond local boundaries.

In relation to *things*, children have a great deal of developing to do. When they are born, their relation to things is entirely ingestive. It is just that they want to absorb anything that can be absorbed, as an amoeba does, in the most primitive way of coping with things. A lot of people continue to be amoebas all their lives, trying to get hold of and incorporate anything they can. Just to have stuff and things is regarded as of itself creditable and productive of a feeling of superiority. A child should be able to be relatively independent of things by the time he goes to school. At least, he should be able to discriminate between things which are just temporarily amusing and those which are really permanently valuable. Again this is a responsibility of his parents.

A child's relationship with *persons* is of such generally recognized importance that it needs no lengthy discussion here. We are all aware that a child's relationship to persons all through his life will be very largely determined during the first weeks and months of his life by his relationship with his mother or the substitute for his mother.

The greatest service that parents can give their children is to help them *to reach reality*, reality as it is known at the present time, and to give them the freedom *to change* this reality—to change their attitudes as more knowledge becomes available, to adjust to changed circumstances without guilt, without feelings of sin, without anxiety and without being afraid to think naturally or to accept their own naturalness. If we can give our children this, then undoubtedly they will be able to become much more mature than we have been or can hope to be because of the handicaps of our particular upbringing.

Bibliography

Chisholm, B. *Prescription for Survival.* New York: Columbia University Press, 1957.

———. *Can People Learn to Learn?* New York: Harper, 1958.

———. "Safe Conformity is Dangerous," *Humanist*, 1959, 19, 323-330.

Fahs, S. L. *Today's Children and Yesterday's Heritage.* Boston: Beacon Press, 1952.

Mondale, L. *Values in World Religions.* Boston: Beacon Press, 1958.

Osgood, P. E. *Religion without Magic.* Boston: Beacon Press, 1954.

Wilson, E. H. "It Starts with Santa Claus," *Humanist*, 1956, 16, 291-297.

10   The Meaning of the Good Life

CARL R. ROGERS

My views regarding the meaning of the good life are
largely based upon my experience in working with people in
the very close and intimate relationship which is called psychotherapy. These views thus have an empirical or experiential foundation, as contrasted perhaps with a scholarly or philosophical foundation. I have learned what the good life seems
to be by observing and participating in the struggle of dis-
turbed and troubled people to achieve that life.

I should make it clear from the outset that this experience I have gained comes from the vantage point of a particular orientation to psychotherapy which has developed over
the years. Quite possibly all psychotherapy is basically similar,
but since I am less sure of that than I once was, I wish to make
it clear that my therapeutic experience has been along the
lines that seem to me most effective—the type of therapy
termed "client-centered."

Let me attempt to give a very brief description of what
this therapy would be like if it were in every respect optimal,
since I feel I have learned most about the good life from therapeutic experiences in which a great deal of movement occurred. If the therapy were optimal, intensive as well as exten-

sive, then it would mean that the therapist has been able to enter into an intensely personal and subjective relationship with the client—relating not as a scientist to an object of study, not as a physician expecting to diagnose and cure but as a person to a person. It would mean that the therapist feels this client to be a person of unconditional self-worth—of value no matter what his condition, his behavior or his feelings. It would mean that the therapist is genuine, hiding behind no defensive facade, but meeting the client with the feelings which organically he is experiencing. It would mean that the therapist is able to let himself go in understanding this client, that no inner barriers keep him from sensing what it feels like to be the client at each moment of the relationship and that he can convey something of his empathic understanding to the client. It means that the therapist has been comfortable in entering this relationship fully, without knowing cognitively where it will lead, satisfied with providing a climate which will provide the client with the utmost freedom to become himself.

For the client, this optimal therapy would mean an exploration of increasingly strange and unknown and dangerous feelings in himself, the exploration proving possible only because he is gradually realizing that he is accepted unconditionally. Thus he becomes acquainted with elements of his experience which have in the past been denied to awareness as too threatening, too damaging to the structure of the self. He finds himself experiencing these feelings fully, completely, in the relationship, so that for the moment he *is* his fear, or his anger, or his tenderness, or his strength. And as he lives these widely varied feelings, in all their degrees of intensity, he discovers that he has experienced *himself*, that he *is* all these feelings. He finds his behavior changing in constructive fashion in accordance with his newly experienced self. He approaches the realization that he no longer needs to fear what experience may hold, but can welcome it freely as a part of his changing and developing self.

In the process of therapy the client sees that some of the main features of his life, especially his values, have originated outside himself rather than inside himself. He sees that he has been trying to live by what others think, that he has not been his true self, and he is less and less satisfied with this situation. Gradually the individual realizes that the evidence upon which he can base a value judgment is supplied by his own senses, his own experience. He discovers that he has within himself the capacity for weighing the experiential evidence and deciding upon those things which make for the long-run enhancement of self and others.

The Good Life As a Process

This, then, is a thumbnail sketch of what client-centered therapy comes close to when it is at its optimum. I give it here simply as a brief picture of the context in which I have formed the view of the good life which is presented in the following paragraphs.

A negative observation

As I have tried to live understandingly in the experiences of my clients I have gradually come to one negative conclusion about the good life. It seems to me that the good life is not any fixed state. It is not, in my estimation, a state of virtue or contentment or nirvana or happiness. It is not a condition in which the individual is adjusted or fulfilled or actualized. To use psychological terms, it is not a state of drive-reduction or tension-reduction or homeostasis.

I believe that all of these terms have been used in ways which imply that if one or several of these states is achieved, then the goal of life has been achieved. Certainly, for many people, happiness or adjustment are seen as states of being which are synonymous with the good life. And social scientists have frequently spoken of the reduction of tension, or the achievement of homeostasis or equilibrium, as if these states constituted the goal of the process of living.

So it is with a certain amount of surprise and concern that I realize that my experience supports none of these definitions. If I focus on the experience of those individuals who seem to have evidenced the greatest degree of movement during the therapeutic relationship and who, in the years following this relationship, appear to have made and to be making real progress toward the good life, then it seems to me that they are not adequately described at all by any of these terms which refer to fixed states of being. I believe they would consider themselves insulted if they were described as "happy" or "contented," or even "actualized." As I have known them I would regard it as most inaccurate to say that all their tensions have been reduced or that they are in a state of homeostasis. So I am forced to ask myself whether there is any way in which I can generalize about their situation, any definition which I can give of the good life which would seem to fit the facts as I have observed them. I find this not at all easy, and what follows is stated very tentatively.

A positive observation

If I attempt to capture in a few words what seems to me to be true of these people, I believe it will come out something like this:

The good life is a *process*, not a state of being.

It is a direction, not a destination.

The direction which constitutes the good life is that which is selected by the total organism, when there is psychological freedom to move in *any* direction.

This organismically selected direction seems to have certain discernible general qualities which appear to be the same in a wide variety of unique individuals.

So I can integrate these statements into a definition which can at least serve as a basis for consideration and discussion. The good life, from the point of view of my experience, is the process of movement in a direction which the human organism selects when it is inwardly free to move in any direction, and the general qualities of this selected direction appear to have a certain universality.

Characteristics of the Process

Let me now try to specify what appear to be the characteristic qualities of this process of movement, as they crop up in person after person in therapy.

An increasing openness to experience

In the first place, the process seems to involve an increasing openness to experience. This phrase has come to have more and more meaning for me. It is the polar opposite of defensiveness. Defensiveness I have described in the past as being the organism's response to experiences which are perceived or anticipated as threatening, as incongruent with the individual's existing picture of himself, or of himself in relationship to the world. These threatening experiences are temporarily rendered harmless by being distorted in awareness, or being denied to awareness. The person quite literally cannot see, with accuracy, those experiences, feelings or reactions in himself which are significantly at variance with the picture of himself which he already possesses. A large part of the process of therapy is the continuing discovery by the client that he is experiencing feelings and attitudes which heretofore he has not been able to be aware of, which he has not been able to "own" as being part of himself.

If a person could be fully open to his experience, however, every stimulus—whether originating within the organism or in the environment—would be freely relayed through the nervous system without being distorted by any defensive mechanism. There would be no need of the mechanism of "subception" whereby the organism is forewarned of any experience threatening to the self. On the contrary, whether the stimulus was the impact of a configuration of form or color or sound in the environment on the sensory nerves, or a memory trace from the past or a visceral sensation of fear or pleasure or disgust, the person would be "living" it, would have it completely available to awareness.

Thus, one aspect of this process which I am naming "the good life" appears to be a movement away from the pole of defensiveness toward the pole of openness to experience. The individual is becoming more able to listen to himself, to experience what is going on within himself. He is more open to his feelings of fear and discouragement and pain. He is also more open to his feelings of courage and tenderness and awe. He is free to live his feelings subjectively, as they exist in him, and is also free to be aware of these feelings. He is more able to live fully the experiences of his organism rather than shutting them out of awareness.

Increasingly existential living

A second characteristic of the process which, for me, is the good life is that it involves an increasing tendency to live fully in each moment. This is a thought which can easily be misunderstood and which is perhaps somewhat vague in my own thinking. Let me try to explain what I mean.

I believe it would be evident that for the person who was fully open to his experience, completely without defensiveness, each moment would be new. The complex configuration of inner and outer stimuli which exists in this moment has never existed before in just this fashion. Consequently such a person would realize that "What I will be in the next moment, and what I will do, grows out of that moment and cannot be predicted in advance either by me or by others." Not infrequently we find clients expressing this sort of feeling.

Thus one, at the end of therapy, says in rather puzzled fashion, "I haven't finished the job of integrating and reorganizing myself, but that's only confusing, not discouraging, now that I realize this is a continuing process. . . . It is exciting, sometimes upsetting, but deeply encouraging to feel yourself in action and apparently knowing where you are going even though you don't always consciously know where that is."

One way of expressing the fluidity which is present in such existential living is to say that the self and personality emerge *from* experience, rather than experience being translated or twisted to fit a preconceived self-structure. It means that one becomes a participant in and an observer of the ongoing process of organismic experience, rather than being in control of it.

Such living in the moment means an absence of rigidity, of tight organization, of the imposition of structure on experience. It means instead a maximum of adaptability, a discovery of structure *in* experience, a flowing, changing organization of self and personality.

It is this tendency toward existential living which appears to me very evident in people who are involved in the process of the good life. One might almost say that it is the most essential quality of it. It involves discovering the structure of experience in the process of living the experience. Most of us, on the other hand, bring a pre-formed structure and evaluation to our experience and never relinquish it, but cram and twist the experience to fit our preconceptions, annoyed at the fluid qualities which make it so unruly in fitting our carefully constructed pigeon-holes. To open one's spirit to what is going on *now*, and to discover in that present process whatever structure it appears to have—this to me is one of the qualities of the good life, the mature life, as I see clients approach it.

An increasing trust in his organism

Still another characteristic of the person who is living the process of the good life appears to be an increasing trust in his organism as a means of arriving at the most satisfying behavior in each existential situation. Again let me try to explain what I mean.

In choosing what course of action to take in any situation, many people rely upon guiding principles, upon the judgment of others (from wife and friends to Emily Post), or upon the way they have behaved in some similar past situation. Yet as I observe the clients whose experiences in living have taught me so much, I find that increasingly such individuals are able to trust their total organismic reaction to a new situation because they discover to an ever-increasing degree that if they are open to their experience, doing what "feels right" proves to be a competent and trustworthy guide to behavior which is truly satisfying.

As I try to understand the reason for this, I find myself following this line of thought. The person who is fully open to his experience would have access to all of the available data in the situation on which to base his behavior—the social demands, his own complex and possibly conflicting needs, his memories of similar situations, his perception of the uniqueness of this situation, etc. The data would be very complex indeed. But he could permit his *total organism*—his consciousness participating—to consider each stimulus, need and demand, its relative intensity and importance, and out of this complex weighing and balancing, discover that course of action which would come closest to satisfying all his needs in the situation.

An analogy which might come close to a description would be to compare this person to a giant electronic computing machine. Since he is open to his experience, all of the data from his sense impressions—from his memory, from previous learning, from his visceral and internal states—is fed into the machine. The machine takes all of these multitudinous pulls and forces which are fed in as data and quickly computes the course of action which would be the most economical vector of need satisfaction in this existential situation. This is the behavior of our hypothetical person.

The defects which in most of us make this process untrustworthy are the inclusion of information which does *not* belong to this present situation, or the exclusion of information which *does*. It is when memories and previous learnings are fed into the computations as if they were *this* reality, and not memories and learnings, that erroneous behavioral answers arise. Or when certain threatening experiences are inhibited from awareness, and hence are withheld from the computation or fed into it in distorted form, this too produces error. But our hypothetical person would find his organism thoroughly trustworthy, because all of the available data would be used, and it would be present in accurate rather than distorted form. Hence his behavior would come as close as possible to satisfying all his needs—for enhancement, for affiliation with others and the like.

In this weighing, balancing and computation, his organism would not by any means be infallible. It would always give the best possible answer for the available data, but sometimes data would be missing. Because of the element of openness to experience, however, any errors, any following of behavior which was not satisfying, would be quickly corrected. The computations, as it were, would always be in process of being corrected because they would be continually checked in behavior.

Perhaps you will not like my analogy of an electronic computing machine. Let me return to the clients I know. As they become more open to all of their experiences, they find it increasingly possible to trust their reactions. If they "feel like" expressing anger they do so and find that this comes out satisfactorily because they are equally alive to all of their other desires for affection, affiliation and relationship. They are surprised at their own intuitive skill in finding behavioral solutions to complex and troubling human relationships. It is only afterward that they realize how surprisingly trustworthy their inner reactions have been in bringing about satisfactory behavior.

The process of functioning more fully

I should like to draw together these three threads describing the process of the good life into a more coherent picture. It appears that the person who is psychologically free moves in the direction of becoming a more fully functioning person. He is more able to live fully in and with each and all of his feelings and reactions. He makes increasing use of all his organic equipment to sense, as accurately as possible, the existential situation within and without. He makes use of all of the information his nervous system can thus supply—using it in awareness but recognizing that his total organism may be, and often is, wiser than his awareness. He is more able to permit his total organism to function freely in all its complexity in selecting, from the multitude of possibilities, that behavior which in this moment of time will be most generally and genuinely satisfying. He is able to put more trust in his organism in this functioning, not because it is infallible, but because he can be fully open to the consequences of each of his actions and correct them if they prove to be less than satisfying.

He is more able to experience all of his feelings, and is less afraid of any of his feelings; he is his own sifter of evidence and is more open to evidence from all sources; he is completely engaged in the process of being and becoming himself, and thus discovers that he is soundly and realistically social; he lives more completely in this moment but learns that this is the soundest living for all time. He is becoming a more fully functioning organism and, because of the awareness of himself which flows freely in and through his experience, he is becoming a more fully functioning person.

Some Implications

Any view of what constitutes the good life carries with it many implications and the perspective I have presented is no exception. I hope that these implications may be food for thought. There are two or three of these about which I would like to comment.

Creativity as an element of the good life

I believe it will be clear that a person who is involved in
the directional process which I have termed "the good life"
is a *creative* person. With his sensitive openness to his world,
his trust of his own ability to form new relationships with his
environment, he would be the type of person from whom
creative products and creative living emerge. He would not
necessarily be "adjusted" to his culture and he would almost
certainly not be a conformist. But at any time and in any culture he would live constructively, in as much harmony with
his culture as a balanced satisfaction of needs demanded. In
some cultural situations he might in some ways be very unhappy, but he would continue to move toward becoming himself and to behave in such a way as to provide the maximum
fulfillment of his values.

Such a person would, I believe, be recognized by the
student of evolution as the type most likely to adapt and survive under changing environmental conditions. He would be
able creatively to make sound adjustments to new as well as
old conditions. He would be a fit vanguard of human evolution.

Basic trustworthiness of human nature

It will be evident that another implication of the view I
have been presenting is that the basic nature of the human being, when functioning freely, is *constructive* and trustworthy.
For me this is an inescapable conclusion from a quarter-cen-

tury of experience in psychotherapy. When we are able to free the individual from defensiveness, so that he is open to the wide range of his own needs—as well as to the wide range of environmental and social demands—his reactions may be trusted to be positive, forward-moving, constructive. We do not have to ask who will socialize him, for one of his own deepest requirements is affiliation and communication with others. As he becomes more fully himself, he will become more realistically socialized.

We do not have to ask who will control his aggressive impulses, for as he becomes more open to all of his impulses, his need to be liked by others and his tendency to give affection will be as strong as his impulses to strike out or to seize for himself. He will be aggressive in situations in which aggression is realistically appropriate but there will be no runaway need for aggression. His total behavior, in these and other areas, as he moves toward being open to all his experience, will be more balanced and realistic—behavior which is appropriate to the survival and enhancement of a highly social animal.

I have little sympathy with the rather prevalent concept that man is basically irrational and that his impulses, if not controlled, will lead to destruction of others and self. Man's behavior is exquisitely rational, moving with subtle and ordered complexity toward the goals his organism is endeavoring to achieve. The tragedy for most of us is that our defenses keep us from being aware of this rationality so that consciously we are moving in one direction while organismically we are moving in another. But in our person who is living the process of the good life there would be *a decreasing number of such bar-*

riers and he would be increasingly a participant in the rationality of his organism.

The only control of impulses which would exist, or which would prove necessary, is the natural and internal balancing of one need against another and the discovery of behaviors which follow the vector most closely approximating the satisfaction of all of the organism's requirements. The experience of extreme satisfaction of one need (for aggression, or sex, etc.) in such a way as to do violence to the satisfaction of other needs (for companionship, tender relationships, etc.)—an experience that is very common in the defensively organized person—would be greatly decreased. He would participate in the vastly complex self-regulatory activities of his organism—the psychological as well as physiological thermostatic controls—in such a fashion as to live in increasing harmony with himself and others.

The greater richness of life

One last implication I should like to mention is that this process of living in the good life involves *a wider range of feelings* than the constricted living in which most of us find ourselves. To be a part of this process means that one is involved in the frequently frightening and frequently satisfying experience of a more sensitive living, with greater variety, greater richness. It seems to me that clients who have moved significantly in therapy live more intimately with their feelings of pain, but also more vividly with their feelings of ecstasy; that anger is more clearly felt, but so also is love; that fear is an experience they know more deeply, but so is courage. And the reason why they can thus live fully in a wider range is that they have this underlying confidence in themselves as trustworthy instruments for encountering life.

I believe it will have become evident why, for me, adjectives such as happy, contented, blissful, enjoyable, do not seem quite appropriate to any general description of this process I have called the good life—even though the person in this process would experience each one of these feelings at appropriate times. But the adjectives which seem more generally fitting are adjectives such as enriching, exciting, rewarding, challenging, meaningful.

This process of the good life is not, I am convinced, a life for the faint-hearted. It involves the stretching and growing of becoming more and more of one's potentialities. It involves *the courage to be*. It means launching oneself fully into the stream of life. It means a continual appraisal of experience and a quest for authentic values. Yet the deeply exciting thing about human beings is that when the individual is inwardly free, he chooses as the good life this process of becoming.

Bibliography

Hayakawa, S. I. "The Fully Functioning Personality," *Etc.*, 1956, 13, 169-181.
Moustakas, C. E. (ed.). *The Self: Explorations in Personal Growth.* New York: Harper, 1956.
Roessler, R. "A Psychiatrist's View of Morality," *Humanist*, 1958, 18, 333-339.
Rogers, C. R. "Significant Aspects of Client-centered Therapy," *American Psychologist*, 1946, 1, 415-422.

———. *Client-centered Therapy*. Boston: Houghton Mifflin, 1951.

———. "Some Directions and End Points in Therapy." In O. H. Mowrer (ed.), *Psychotherapy, Theory and Research*. New York: Ronald Press, 1953. Pp. 44-68.

———. "A Theory of Therapy, Personality, and Interpersonal Relationships." In S. Koch (ed.), *Psychology: A Study of a Science*. Vol. 3. New York: McGraw-Hill, 1959. Pp. 184-256.

———. *A Therapist's View of Personal Goals*. Pamphlet #108. Wallingford, Pa.: Pendle Hill, 1960.

Part V   Fulfillment

11   Human Wealth and Economic Growth

THEODORE W. SCHULTZ

We Americans have traditionally taken it for granted that expansion, growth—particularly economic growth—is in itself a good thing. But recently we have witnessed the beginnings of a debate; it is being argued that we are putting too much emphasis on economic growth in national policy and in our thinking, and that it should be given a lower priority. This essentially is the thesis of a book by Professor John K. Galbraith of Harvard, *The Affluent Society*. In effect, Galbraith closes the United States off and says that we have grown fairly rich now, and why then be concerned about more economic growth?

This amounts to a very sophisticated new brand of isolationism with which I would quarrel seriously, and I was glad to see an article by Leon Keyserling in which he took Galbraith and others very much to task for this limited view. Mr. Keyserling said very effectively—not speaking as an economist, and more effectively than an economist could have said it—that if we were truly aware of our responsibility in the world today, we would see that we are indeed very poor.

This is not to argue that economic growth will necessarily solve all the problems of the world. It cannot give us all the necessary and sufficient conditions for world peace. Nor is rapid economic growth always a comfortable process for the countries involved. Very heavy stresses and strains are implicit in the changes brought by rapid growth in the economy. We in the West do not usually consider this when we urge poor countries to move ahead more rapidly. But it is easier to see at home, for example in American agriculture, where change has been so rapid that the social cost is very high.

During just one peacetime year, from April 1956 to April 1957, two million people left American agriculture. That was 10 per cent of the American farm population. In leaving this sector of the economy, these people normally had to change both location and job, giving up not only their occupation but their community life as well. When change occurs at such a fantastic rate, the social cost is proportionately high. And we should bear in mind that when rapid growth occurs in poor countries, the same kind of thing happens. This is not to argue against economic growth but to say that order, too, has value for the community, that order and change should each have a place in the thinking and experience of communities where change is going on.

What then, we may ask, do people want economic growth for? Do people, as individuals and as communities, *want* economic growth? Is it important to them, and why? My answer is that economic growth is important on a world-wide scale because there is so much poverty in the world. And we no longer believe that poverty is ordained by God. Men today will not be kept down in poverty because it is a part of the symbolism of a caste or class or religion. Men *can*, and men *will*, do something about it.

The example of early industrial development in the West, of Japan later on and Russia more recently, has become common knowledge all over the world. People in the areas we think of as "backward"—Africa, some of the Asian countries, even the Indians in the mountains of Peru—are rapidly becoming informed and aware of these vital matters. They want first-class citizenship and the right to enjoy some of the fruits of living, and not the bare subsistence that for centuries has been their lot.

Economic growth, therefore, is important both for us here in the United States and for others; and it is important for us to comprehend the way in which it is brought about. I believe that we in America do not really understand our own economic growth and how it was achieved. Much of our debate on the subject is in terms of material as against spiritual values. And we think of economics as materialistic, partly because we have identified capital with goods—reproducible goods—and have not seen it in its human context. This applies to Marxian theory as well as to our own non-Marxian thinking.

At the individual level, the way to achieve economic growth can be stated very simply: work and save. You work hard, you are thrifty and save and you accumulate something called "capital." It helps to have chosen your birthplace wisely —to be born where there is plenty of oil, and coal, ores, rich farm lands, harbors and rivers; but I suspect that this is less important than has been supposed. Consider the prosperity of landlocked, mountainous Switzerland; or look at what the Puerto Ricans are doing on an island that has almost no resources, or take Mexico, which is far from rich in this sense.

And there are other examples. The key to economic development, I believe, is in *man himself*, and not in material resources.

Another road to economic growth has been revolution—followed by a generation or two of enforced accumulation of capital, achieved by forced labor of one kind or another along with drastic limits on consumption. The human cost of that road is, of course, appalling. It is shown in Boris Pasternak's much-discussed novel, *Dr. Zhivago*, where we see the lives of a few people who try to save their souls from the crushing excesses of a vast revolution. Similar excesses characterized the French Revolution and also, in some ways, the Mexican Revolution. It would be a mistake to see Pasternak's novel as a purely political document, rather than as an account of what happens to human values during such a revolution. William Faulkner's account of other human values in *Intruder in the Dust*, with its setting in American society, is if anything sharper and more devastating than anything in *Dr. Zhivago*.

Causes of Economic Growth

Let us consider economic growth in the United States and how it came about. Do the increases in man-hours of labor—the total man-hours worked as our population and labor force have grown—plus the increases in the stock of real capital, account for most or all of our own economic growth throughout our history? Several recent studies have been made that bear on this question and they all tell very much the same story.

Consider the period from 1929 to 1953, which is fairly

recent and avoids some of the measurement problems that would be met if we went back further. During this time, the total national real income of this country—and by real income we mean not money income but "real things"—a little more than doubled. If we think of it in terms of compound interest, this is an increase of something more than 3 per cent per year.

During the above period, while total real income doubled, our resources in terms of total man-hours in the labor force increased by 17 per cent. At the same time, the total capital stock—that is, the value of material resources, manufacturing plants, etc.—went up 42 per cent. If these figures are weighted properly, the total rise in input (man-hours and capital stock combined) is about one-third—or, in compound interest terms, an increase of 1.2 per cent per year as compared with the 3 per cent increase in real income.

The increase in resources, then, would seem to account for about two-fifths of the rise in real income, leaving three-fifths open and to be explained. We added a third to our resources and ended up with twice the product. Where did the rest come from? What explains the difference? This is the enigma of our history; we do not understand it ourselves, and I think most of the political debate on this issue is quite beside the point. Both the liberal and the conservative views on economic growth are probably wrong.

Businessmen and others who tend to the conservative view would probably argue that if we want more rapid growth in the American economy we will have to give larger incentives to people to "hustle," to work, save, invest, accumulate capital, build new plants and so on. Lower taxes on these activities might provide these incentives. And conservatives would also argue, no doubt, that when government decisions result in waste of resources, these decisions should be corrected. A fair case might be made here in connection with, for example, some of the transportation decisions made by the Interstate Commerce Commission and some of our agricultural policies. If, however, as we have just seen, growth in capital accounts for such a small proportion of total growth, it would seem impossible that even substantially higher incentives to increase capital in reproducible goods would result in a substantially greater increase in total growth.

On the liberal side, our friends in labor would say that to get rapid growth we should reduce unemployment; that if, instead of running 5 to 6 per cent unemployment on the average, we could get this figure down to 3 or even 2 per cent as they are doing in some European countries, the problem would be solved. Certainly this would result in a larger product in the beginning; there would be a rise when the extra resources in human effort were "allowed" to work. But it does not follow that this would lead to a higher *rate* of growth from then on, and the picture in European countries at present bears this out. I do not mean to argue that a decrease in unemployment is not a desirable thing to achieve; but it cannot by itself bring about economic growth of the explosive kind shown in the unexplained figures just given.

Another argument of the liberals is that the public sector of the economy should be enlarged, more resources being given to the government to spend in certain ways, in order to achieve this kind of rapid growth. Of course, the list of things that ought to be done on the public account is a very long one: urban renewal in our large cities; enlargement of social security; conservation of natural resources; improving our parks, rivers and harbors; development of water resources, dams,

power; building highways, schools and hospitals; and so on.
But even if each of these were increased by 20 per cent,
I doubt that this would lead to appreciably more economic
growth. Certainly we are woefully behind in some public facilities in our society today and, for the welfare of our citizens,
we should be spending more funds on these things. But I do
not believe a case has been made for the achievement of economic growth in this way.

Formation of Human Capital

What then is the key to economic growth? The hypothesis which follows has become the center of my own work
in studying this subject, and I do not wish to state it as dog-
matically proven, but it seems to organize the relevant facts of
our history and experience better than any other hypothesis
I have worked with.

That hypothesis can be stated this way: Looking at our
own economic growth from 1929 to 1953, or at the rapid
growth of Japan or Germany or other countries, one observes
what I shall call an under-specification of resources. We have
not taken into account one of the principal forms of wealth,
and the additions that have been made in that sphere, and my
thesis is that the part we have left out of the whole picture is
our increasing stock of *human* wealth. This human wealth
consists of improvements in human effectiveness arising from
the fact that man has developed capabilities that result from
investments in man.

We may feel a bit touchy at having this concept of "capital" taken over from the realm of reproducible, material things

and applied to ourselves as humans. And yet perhaps the greatest capital formation that has been going on in our society is this investment *in ourselves*. It may be that these investments in ourselves—in our abilities, our talents and capacities, in our stamina, our health, the way we live and what we eat—are the very kinds of capital that make the greatest returns in terms of reward for our efforts.

One aspect of this human wealth, of course, is the great increase in useful knowledge. I first became aware of the importance of this when I tried to understand the rapid growth that has taken place in some parts of Latin America. Mexico, for example, has been an extraordinarily poor country. If anyone had told me, when I first studied it in 1930, that Mexico could achieve the increase in output—in its total production—that it has achieved since that time I should have said it would be impossible. Particularly I should have said this about the economic area I knew best, agriculture. If I had been told that Mexico, with its pitifully poor resources, could actually double its output in agriculture—traditionally one of the hardest kinds of output to increase—I should have denied it. But that is what the Mexicans have done. Their gross national product has been rising by 7 or 8 per cent a year, but the agricultural product has been rising even faster. Since 1947 they have had an increase in gross national product of approximately 80 per cent, and they have again *doubled* their output in agriculture! Similar things, although less dramatic, have been happening in Brazil and in other places—such as Puerto Rico.

These observations prompted a second look at some earlier work in which I had found that in this country, since 1923, for every 25 per cent increase in agricultural output, we had increased our input in man-hours and material resources by no more than 3 to 5 per cent. It suddenly occurred to me that some of these countries that are moving forward so rapidly now are doing much the same thing. They have found a way to get a greatly increased output without an input that is proportionately large. This would appear to be a direct contradiction of the doctrine of the eighteenth-century economists, Ricardo and Malthus, who held that for every increase of, say 10 per cent in input, a country would get somewhat less than 10 per cent growth in output—the classic image of "diminishing returns."

In order to discover just what was going on in these areas, my students and I began a series of studies—particularly of Argentina, Mexico and Brazil. These studies showed that Brazil and Mexico in particular began to develop, in the late twenties, and achieved an increase in agricultural output that was substantially greater than the additional input. Argentina showed a pattern of growth that looked very much like that of Canada and the United States, until Perón came to power, and then reversed itself. Unfortunately, Argentina has not begun to move forward again even now, three years after Perón's downfall.

In another study, I then undertook to try to discover whether these unexplained, omitted "inputs" could be represented as the return on the investment that has been going into humans. One of these investments is education—in high schools, colleges and graduate schools in the United States. Comparing figures for two dates, 1920 and 1956, we can identify what economists would call gross capital formation, in ourselves, for this one kind of investment during that period. In 1920, counting all the costs as you would if you were developing capital in the physical sense, our investment in this education in the United States was 1.5 billion dollars. In 1956 this figure had risen to 20.9 billion dollars. This is a much more rapid increase than the value of our physical capital during the same period. In fact, it was 7 per cent of gross physical capital in 1920 and in 1956 it was up to 25 per cent.

And even this is an understatement. In terms of net capital (that is, the life of capital when its depreciation is subtracted) the comparison is even more striking, because during this period the life of human capital has been increasing very substantially. A person invests in himself and then has a longer period of useful activity in society than he would have had some thirty years ago. At the same time, the life of so-called physical capital is getting shorter and shorter. This is one of the notable phenomena of our time.

Investments in Education

The individual and social returns on our investments in education are suggested in the results of a recent study in which Morton Zeman, in his doctoral research at the University of Chicago, tried to explain the very large differences in the average earnings of urban workers—Negro and white. Using census figures, Zeman was able to classify people—white and Negro—by region, city size, age and education. He found that in the North, comparing Negro and white workers all of whom had had five years of school, the average difference in their earnings was small. The average earnings of Northern Negroes were slightly less than those of whites of the same education level.

Of course there are other factors influencing earning

power—such as age, city size and so on—and in the South the picture is still more complex. But the extraordinary thing was that, at any rate in the North, the most important factor determining the differences in earning power of white and Negro workers was the amount of education they had. This suggests that one of the tragic errors in American history has been our failure to invest in Negroes as citizens as we have invested in whites as citizens. One of the great costs has been the lower productivity in the economy, as well as the individual differences in earnings as revealed by Dr. Zeman.

Other studies, of white and Negro farm families, have yielded similar results. The implication is that our economy pays high rewards for more investment in people, as shown even by this crude measure. The fifth year in school, the sixth year in school, the seventh and eighth and on through the high schools—with each added year of education the rewards increase.

The social returns on investment in new, useful knowledge are demonstrated in another set of studies. In a project underwritten by the National Science Foundation, we attempted to identify particular pieces of new knowledge that have moved into the economy, and to see what they cost the society and what return they made to the society. One such piece of new knowledge that we were able to isolate and treat in this way was the development of hybrid corn.

The history of hybrid corn development in this country goes back to 1910, with relatively few people involved at first, but with a pyramiding of effort in the later stages. A colleague of mine, Professor Griliches, has recently published the results of some very ingenious research. He has found that if we count all of the private and public costs of hybrid corn, everything that has gone into its development—and the records on this are quite complete—a total of 130 million dollars has been invested since 1910. (This figure also allows for compound interest of 10 per cent over the time period, but that is a technicality.) Then if we measure all of the product that can be identified and attributed to this particular new piece of useful knowledge, we find that its contribution to the consumer surplus—and it quickly becomes a consumer surplus, which is what made the analysis so difficult and required so much ingenuity—turns out to be no less than 900 million dollars. That is, the annual return on the 130 million dollars invested is running close to 700 per cent per year!

Most of the time we consider it an improvement if we can work out an allocation of resources that increases the return from 5 per cent to 6 per cent. We criticize private or public business if they are sinking funds in 5 per cent areas when they could use such resources in activities that produce 6, 7 or 8 per cent. My argument is that we should be looking for ways in which human effort and useful knowledge can move us into the range of 50 per cent, 100, 200—even 700 per cent return. This is the key to the explosion of our own economic wellbeing.

If my hypothesis is correct, it carries radical implications for our thinking about the rest of the world. It implies that fewer steel mills and other big plants should be built in the underdeveloped countries and that more should be invested in *the people* of those countries, as we have invested in ourselves.

As we look at other countries, let me draw a few comparisons. We can now gain new insights into why Great Britain's growth has been appreciably slower than our own during the past fifty years. The British have neglected the edu-

cation of the middle group in their society. Their elementary-
education system is much like ours, perhaps better. But at
what we call the secondary-school level, before university education begins, the story is of two different worlds. Our secondary schools, like the elementary schools in both countries, still
deal in mass education. At this level we are investing in people on a mass basis. In Britain, on the contrary, only some 15
to 18 per cent of the people go beyond elementary school.

By way of contrast, let us look at Japan, to take a highly
populated, Asiatic country. Something happened in Japan at
a very early date, and it began to produce not only industrial
products but also much more food under the most adverse circumstances. The agricultural achievements of Japan between
1875 and 1910—before World War I—stand as a miracle. In
1873 Japan moved to universal education—a six-year program
compulsory all over the country. As a result, it very soon had
a literate population. The rural people became more skilled at
farming, and a supply of more sophisticated labor was made
available to industry, more sophisticated than even European
countries had at that time, and far more so than that of other
Asiatic countries. We should remember that we did not have
compulsory education for Negroes or for some whites in the
United States at that time.

I think I now understand why Japanese tenant farmers
could come to our West Coast and do better at farming than
many American farmers with whom they were competing. It
is often said that they were able to save and buy land because
they were willing to accept lower standards of living. But that
is not the whole story. I have seen some of these farms. I remember one, of 231 acres, not far from Stanford, which had
been acquired by a thrifty Japanese tenant who came over in

the late twenties. He and his family farmed the land intensively, with little extra labor—about ten people in all at peak periods—and today he is an American citizen, owns his farm and his three sons are all graduates of the University of California. When I visited him, he was selling over half a million dollars' product a year from 231 acres. The intricacy of that farming operation makes our agriculture in most of the United States look simple.

A parallel situation would be the postwar recovery of West Germany. When I saw the destruction of the houses, the factories—whole cities in ruins—like everyone else, even the Germans themselves, I missed completely in anticipating the rate of recovery. We simply could not visualize what would happen in growth—in production—during the next decade, or up to the present. And the reason was that we were putting too much emphasis on steel mills, plants, machinery, railroads and buildings. We didn't see *the human capital*—and it was the human capital that went to work.

Alone on the High Road?

What does all this mean for United States policy? I believe it means that the time has come when we have to understand ourselves, and recognize the predominant role of human capital, human wealth. Somehow we have hit on a productive formula for our own society; and it seems that the Russians also are making large gains on this score. The importance of the role of new physical capital in the Soviet Union is often overstressed. The Russians, like ourselves, have been creating human capital very rapidly; and they have been turning it sharply and directly to economic account—undoubtedly at the expense of values we hold dear in our own free society.

Therefore, as we take a hand and act responsibly in other countries, we should bear in mind that the increase in real earnings—the rise in product that is needed to help the peoples of the world out of their poverty—requires human capital. Whether it be in Point Four technical assistance programs, in activities like the Rockefeller Foundation work in Mexico with hybrid corn, in the work of church groups operating through some sixteen hundred mission projects in agriculture, education and health in Latin America and elsewhere, or through private business—the transfer and development of *new knowledge* and *new capabilities* are the most important contributions we can make. This is where the underdeveloped countries tend to neglect themselves. The great neglect in India, for example, is *men*. There are now three countries in Africa that are investing more per capita in human resources in this generation than India is. The great emphasis on human capital in Puerto Rico makes it stand out in comparison with other Latin American countries.

We in the United States stand here on the high road, which is indeed well paved with large stocks of knowledge and many developed abilities. This is our good fortune, part of our heritage and history. But is this road for us alone? What about most of mankind, trudging on the low road marked "poverty," working so hard and with so little knowledge? I believe we will not want to leave them there in the condition which Faulkner portrays in his description of the lonely cultivator: "The man and the mule and the wooden plow, which coupled them furious and solitary, leaning terrifically against nothing."

Bibliography

Griliches, Z. "Research Costs and Social Returns: Hybrid Corn and Related Innovations." *Journal of Political Economy*, 1958, 66, 419-431.

Keyserling, L. "Eggheads and Politics." *New Republic*, 1958, 139:17, 13-17.

Moore, C. A. "Agricultural Development in Mexico." *Journal of Farm Economics*, 1955, 37, 72-80.

———. "Recent Developments in Brazilian Agriculture." *Journal of Political Economy*, 1956, 64, 341-346.

Schultz, T. W. "Reflections on Agricultural Production, Output and Supply." *Journal of Farm Economics*, 1956, 38, 748-762.

———. "Investment in Man: An Economist's View." *Social Service Review*, 1959, 33, 109-117.

———. "Capital Formation by Education." *Journal of Political Economy*, 1960, 68, 571-583.

12   The Richer Rich and Poorer Poor

SAMUEL JACOBS

The American people went into the Marshall Plan easily and naturally. The appeal was simple and fitted American humanitarian impulses, particularly because the plan served primarily countries that suffered from a war in which we had been on the winning side.

Compared with the job of economic development in the countries of Asia, Africa and Latin America, the European problem was an easy one. The countries involved had already been industrialized; they needed only to be rebuilt. Their cultures were technological and thus similar to ours. The intricate structure of attitudes, motivations and behavior patterns needed for twentieth-century industrial living was in place, complementing our own and matching our readiness to give with a readiness to receive.

In the short time that the plan was in operation, recovery was rapid. In Germany it was dramatic, even startling. It was clear that our international aid program was related to something that worked.

For the countries whose problems of economic emergence now confront us, what has to be done is infinitely more complicated. The cultural difference between them and us is much greater; so is the difference in living levels. For instance, while the per capita income in the United States during the 1952-1954 period was three and a half times as high as that in Germany, it was eight times as high as that in Brazil and more than nine times as high as that in Japan.

The median per capita income for fifty-four countries of the world studied by the UN for the 1952-1954 period was approximately $445, about a fourth of the income in this country at that time and approximately what it was here a hundred years ago. Only Venezuela, Argentina and Israel—of all the countries of Africa, Asia and Latin America—were above the world-wide median.

In the face of these differences, the task of helping to raise living standards in these countries is big enough in absolute terms. Raising them faster than we raise our own, to narrow the gap between us, provides an intimidating problem in economics and a severe challenge to international morality.

Far from yielding to time and the effort that has already been made, the gap between the industrialized and the non-industrialized countries is widening, and particularly the gap between the United States and most of the rest of the world. In 1938 this country had about 6 per cent of the world's population and about 26 per cent of the world's income. By 1949 our share of the population had increased to 6.5 per cent, but our share of the income had jumped to 41 per cent.

In Asia, on the other hand, the share of the world's population had declined somewhat, from 53 per cent in 1938 to 52 per cent in 1949. However, in the same period, Asia's share of the world's income had declined from 17 per cent to 11 per cent.

In Africa the story was a little different, but the ending

was very much the same. That is, while the share of the world's population increased from 7 per cent in 1938 to 9 per cent in 1949, the African share of the world's income dropped slightly.

The Effects of Automation

The trend toward richer rich and poorer poor—certainly as far as relative position is concerned—has been continuing. Dr. Kingsley Davis has pointed out that "fifteen of the richest industrial countries in 1938 had an average per capita income roughly ten times that of the twenty non-industrialized countries. In 1952-1954 the same industrial countries had an average per capita income about eleven times that of the same non-industrial countries."

It is not in relation to industrialization alone that the problem presents itself. In agriculture, too, there is a problem to be met, and it is not being met well. The Foreign Agricultural Service of the United States Department of Agriculture has reported that the world's agricultural production has been barely keeping up with the increase in population. Surpluses here are matched by deficits in other places.

Technological developments in American industry promise that the gap will continue to widen. American industry is adopting automation. Production is increasing, while hundreds of thousands of our workers are being set free to do other things. (It is not at all clear yet that we shall have the wit to put these people to work producing other things; there is still the possibility that these displaced workers will constitute a large group of permanently unemployed, making no contribution in the economic system of America. Nevertheless, the concern in other countries—both the industrialized and the nonindustrialized—with the consequences of this new industrial revolution in America is great.)

Recently UNESCO's *International Social Science Bulletin* devoted an issue to "The Social Consequences of Automation." From the many statements of concern with what is happening as a result of automation, it is hard to select the quotes that typify the rest. However, the following statement by the leader of the Yugoslav delegation to ECOSOC may serve:

The new technological revolution which is now taking place before our eyes will not, of itself, contribute towards a more balanced economic development of the world. Automation and nuclear energy, these two main achievements of contemporary technology, are already being applied in the developed countries on an ever-increasing scale. The increase in the productivity of labour, achieved through the introduction of modern technology, is assuming sometimes overwhelming proportions. . . .

All this new technology is concentrated in the countries which have already the highest income, the largest capital formation and the highest productivity of labour.

Automation and modern techniques, which are used in the developed countries, enable these countries to reduce constantly their production costs and at the same time to expand mass production in unheard-of proportions. This obviously places the economies of the countries which are making efforts towards an overall economic development in an ever more difficult position. This new disadvantage can no longer be met in underdeveloped countries by the old devices of pressure on wages.

In other words, this development of technology is a new element which tends to widen the already existing gap between the developed and underdeveloped areas of the world.

Prime Minister Nehru of India complained to the joint conference of the international development finance agencies that, in the developed countries, "the pace of progress through the development of science and technology is tremendous," while for countries like India "it is a struggle for survival."

Underdeveloped countries, such as Yugoslavia and India, are not the only ones concerned. The same concern is felt in countries that are definitely our technological contemporaries, if not our economic equals—Sweden, for example.

Over the past few years, the growth in Sweden's national income has been most impressive. The increase in per capita income, resulting from the more rapid increase in income than in population, has exceeded ours by a considerable margin, in percentage terms. In 1952-1954 Sweden stood next to Switzerland, with the second highest per capita income among the countries of Europe—at about 50 per cent of the per capita income in the United States!

Now, Swedish observers view American technological development with deep concern. To change over to automated production methods as in this country would be tremendously expensive. Corporations such as General Motors and U. S. Steel can take these huge outlays in their colossuslike stride. But few other countries of the world can marshal the great sums, which flow so readily in America, to pay for rapid automation of industry. Even Sweden will find it hard to keep up with American progress and may have to see the gap, which it has worked so hard to narrow, widening again.

And if this is true of Sweden, how much more is it true of the countries of Africa, Asia and Latin America.

Population Pressure

Obviously, the problem is not alone with the economic factor; the population problem is one side of the coin, the other side of which is production of goods and services. That the rich get richer while *the poor get children* may be an inelegant way of saying it, but it does express one of the crucial realities in the international economic development problem.

Whether or not the Malthusians are right about the inadequacy of the world's resources for larger populations, there is an inescapable, Micawber-like arithmetic that must be taken into account in considering the immediate increase in per capita incomes. It confronted America in the late 1700s, when population increased rapidly through immigration, and the national income increased slowly—if at all—held down by, among other things, the suspension of trade during the Napoleonic wars. It implacably confronts the emerging countries of the world today. As Dr. Davis put it in the comparison referred to previously: "Over the period covered, 1938 to 1952-1954, the population of the fifteen industrial countries rose by 7.6 per cent; that of the non-industrial countries by 10.7 per cent. If the rates of human multiplication had been reversed, national income remaining the same, the gap between the two groups in per capita income would have been narrowed rather than widened."

The problem can be put simply in this way: Only when the increase in production is greater than the increase in population can living standards rise. For many years American output of goods and services increased by about 4 per cent per year, and population increased by about 1.5 per cent per year. Under these circumstances, part of the increase in production could be diverted into new plant and equipment—seed for even further increases—and still leave plenty of room for an increase in the production of consumer goods to take care of the increase in population and to increase living levels for everybody.

This nice fat margin of production over population increase is not typical of the world, however. In Brazil, for example, the increase in production has been approximately as high as ours. However, the population increase has run at approximately 3 per cent per year. In this kind of situation, a country is lucky to hold its own. Any effort to get ahead of the game may result in lowering living standards for at least a time, and governments fall for less than that.

Brazilian spokesmen have proposed that the Latin countries, whose average per capita incomes at the time was $312 per year, should embark on a drive to raise those incomes to an average of $480 by 1980. With population increasing at an average rate of 2 per cent per year, to accomplish this goal would require a production increase of 4.5 per cent per year— a truly heroic effort. Success in such an undertaking would require large foreign loans, increased private investment, control over inflation and increased exports to Russia and China. It will be interesting to see how the drive works out, if it is indeed undertaken.

The investment in plant and equipment to bring about any such goal as Brazil is discussing would have to be great. It has been estimated that the underdeveloped countries of the world ought to be increasing their capital investment at the rate of 10 to 12 per cent per year to get a proper hold on the problem; it is actually running somewhat less than half that amount. Some years ago the UN estimated that to raise the per capita incomes of the underdeveloped countries by 2 per cent per year would require that these countries get 10 billion dollars per year from outside their own resources, 3 billion dollars of it in grants. This would work if these countries made much better use of their own savings than they now make and it would double their living standards in thirty-five years.

A complicating problem, however, is the fact that in some countries the rate of population increase may well become greater over the years immediately ahead. In India, for example, the rate of population increase today is about 1.5 per cent per year—not a high rate as rates go. However, this rate of increase is so low because the death rate is so high. With better sanitation and improved economic conditions, the death rate can be expected to go down, and the population can be expected to increase still faster. Further, the UN has stated, in the countries in which the birth rates are now high, the trend is toward even higher birth rates—so a decline in death rates will have truly explosive effects.

Left to itself, the population problem will naturally come under control, but very slowly. In Europe the death rate went down for more than fifty years before the birth rate began to fall. Even though whatever happens, happens faster these days than it used to, it is doubtful that the natural decline in birth rates will do very much to solve the problem in the near future.

What the United States can do to help with this problem

in the very short run is hard to see. But certainly whatever can be done to encourage the educational efforts now under way in many of the countries that have this problem must be done.

American Fears

In the meantime, the voices of despair are heard in America. In August 1958, for example, a distinguished United States senator took the floor to argue that the American people "would not stomach" an extended program of international aid to the underdeveloped countries of the world. The President had long argued that the burden of the Cold War made it impossible for us to do more than we were doing. Read the current statements; what they amount to is that the world must first disarm. Then we must reduce taxes—and that on corporations and high incomes—before we can do more than we are now doing.

It is on this basis that the proposal to set up the Special UN Fund for Economic Development (SUNFED) has been kept in deep freeze since 1951. Since our objection was based on our plea that we could not afford to contribute to it, the proposal has even been denied the opportunity of proper debate—in which its merits and demerits might have been worked out. Yet in recent months the United States has agreed to go along with a small-sized fund, intended to keep the underdeveloped areas safe for American private investors who, however, at least so far, have been able to find plenty of opportunity to use their money at home in highly profitable ways.

The approach we take to this problem persuades the American people to an irrational fear that we have not the economic strength to hold up our end of the job that has to be done. Americans are persuaded that we are *too poor* to contribute our share; a great many people really believe that economic disaster will result from our making a contribution to world economic development commensurate with the size of the job that must be done.

But even more persuasive than the predictions of domestic debility are the recurring recessions and the economic insecurity that they induce. Even in so-called prosperous times, the government's official list of the economically distressed areas contains the names of many of the country's populous industrial and mining centers—many of them embracing large cities and a wide radius of the surrounding country. In more congressional districts than the American people are aware of, hundreds of thousands of American workers are counted as persistently and continuously unemployed. Even when the rest of the country is doing well, no one knows when jobs will be available for these men and women. And in many areas it is not difficult to relate unemployment to economic competition from abroad, or to draw the lesson that this is what aid to economic development abroad may mean for other areas of our own country.

Certainly to a worker whose unemployment compensation benefits have been cut off because he has been unemployed too long, for whom there is now nothing left but welfare as long as the welfare funds hold out, it makes sense to believe that charity ought to begin at home. To the nine million families in which someone was unemployed some of the time in recent months, to the businessmen whose stores have closed during the same period and to the many millions who learn from the experiences of these people, the arguments against international aid must sound impressive. At best their experience leads them to listen sympathetically to the arguments for caution and constriction rather than for courage and imagination. Since we have never allowed our people to understand how rich this country really can be, it is hard to convince them that, at worst, an adequate international program would only slow down somewhat the rate at which our economy is becoming even richer and fatter.

How Rich We Could Be

Here is one way to show what is happening. In 1957 the high per capita income of this country resulted from the fact that the average employed person produced at the rate of $6,500 per year—a truly impressive output of goods and services. A conservative private research organization has published an estimate that, in effect, forecasts production in 1975 at the rate of $9,500 per employed person (at present prices), a most impressive increase—yet based on truly conservative assumptions. The increase in per capita income and in living standards that can result from even this increase in ability to produce is tremendous, if we have the wit to keep the production going. In other words, according to this research service, in 1975 our gross national product could reach 835 billion dollars instead of the 440 billion dollars of 1957—an increase of more than 20 billion dollars per year.

How conservative this estimate is, is shown by the conclusions reached in the Rockefeller Report that in this country "a growth rate of 5 per cent is possible if we realize fully our impressive opportunities for economic expansion. If the problems of growth are formidable, we have also found the impetus of our economy enormous."

A growth rate of 5 per cent would give us an output of approximately 1,100 billion dollars in 1975 instead of the 835 billion dollars estimated in the forecast referred to above. What a tremendous burden of guilt must be ours as we face the people of the world, knowing *how little we are doing* compared with what our resources permit us to do!

Now, the UN estimate of the amount of outside capital required by the underdeveloped countries worked out to about 2 per cent of the annual production of the industrialized countries at that time. If we were now to accept the responsibility for contributing 2 per cent of our total production to international development—approximately nine billion dollars per year—this large sum would be no more than half the potential *increase* in our output during the first year. If the arrangement were kept up, in 1975 the production per employed worker available to us for our own use on the basis of the more conservative estimates would be $9,300 instead of the predicted $9,500. We would have increased the domestic benefits of increased producing power by 43 per cent instead of the predicted 46 per cent.

Indeed, there is poverty at home and we must take steps to eliminate it. In 1957, about 6.5 per cent of American families had incomes of less than $1,000. A total of nearly 25 per cent of our families had incomes below $3,000. Past studies indicate that if the figures were available to measure the cost of the "City Worker's Family Budget," they almost certainly would show that the average family income—$4,971—was not enough to pay for this far from ideal level of living.

Certainly by far the major part of this increase in per person production ought to go into raising the living standards of these low income families. More money ought to go into health, education and many other services. But this increase in the gross national welfare need not be given up in order to help the emerging countries.

Certainly our ability to provide food for our people, schools for our own children, factories for our growing labor force would in no way be endangered. Yet what a force on earth America might become, what a stimulation to the solution of the world's economic difficulties could be accomplished!

A Moral Revolution

Yet our inability to create such a program—if we are indeed unable to do so at this time—is not the result of economic conditions. It is not because our soil will not produce or our factories are inadequate to the job. The problem is more difficult than that, and the work to be done is more difficult than the simple task of inventing new machinery, devising new technologies and harnessing new sources of power.

To do the job, the American people must create *a revolution in their own thinking*. They must refuse to go on living under the false pall of insecurity and the fear of their own good impulses that now determine policy in the field of international aid. They must come to understand how much America could produce for our own and world consumption if our economy were set free to do the job. They must demand to be told what ways of housekeeping must be installed so that the productive power of America may be geared up to the needs of the world, instead of being kept cramped and constricted while a world of people go in want for lack of what we will not produce. They must then insist that these new housekeeping methods be incorporated into national policy.

The failure to solve this problem not only cheats us of billions of dollars worth of production we ought to have for our own use and enjoyment, for the elimination of widespread poverty in our own nation. It also discredits us doubly in the eyes of the world—for our failure to recognize our opportunities to assist with the job of economic development, and for our inability to solve the housekeeping problems on which full employment and continued economic growth depend.

There is one American product that we have ready for instant export: *universal public education*, the magic ingredient of our own phenomenal growth. The effect of this ingredient in stimulating economic development was described recently at a regional conference of the American Humanist Association by Professor Theodore W. Schultz, who pointed out that possibly 50 per cent of the economic growth taking place in this country after 1870 can be accounted for by *our investment in people*—by the money spent on education and on health, particularly on the former.

Had we endorsed SUNFED when it was first proposed in 1951, the investment in the people of the underdeveloped countries in health, education and economic plant would now be over ten years ahead of where it now is—for that is what the plan called for.

The world needs a revolution, not just to oppose communism but to help create *human dignity and freedom*. It needs the kind of revolution that can be fashioned in school-rooms, factories and mills. This is the kind of revolution that Americans know a great deal about. But, if it is to take place, it must begin with a revolution in our own thinking that will make Americans aware of the vital role that we can play in creating a world-wide upsurge in human accomplishment. In economic terms, such a change in our perspective is essential if the American giant is to reach full strength for the economic job that must be done to help set the people of the world free.

There is still time for us to wake up to our opportunities, but there is no time to spare.

Bibliography

Crozier, M., *et al.* "Social Consequences of Automation." *International Social Science Bulletin*, 1958, 10, 1-120.

Davis, K. "The Political Impact of New Population Trends." *Foreign Affairs*, 1958, 36, 293-301.

Rockefeller, N. A., *et al. The Challenge to America: Its Economic and Social Aspects.* New York: Doubleday, 1958.

13   Poverty and Population

FRANK W. NOTESTEIN

Mankind has the technical ability to reduce the toll of sickness and poverty throughout the world to an extent never dreamed of even a few decades ago. Yet we teeter on the brink of self-destruction by allowing population growth to outstrip economic advance.

Both in the modernized countries and in the underdeveloped areas themselves there is much discussion, debate and controversy over the population problem—but little action has been taken. Part of the controversy arises from honest and probably inevitable differences in moral judgments. But a larger part arises from misunderstandings both here and in the areas involved.

The problem is most intense in those parts of the world where average incomes are barely above the minimum of subsistence, where illiteracy is prevalent, where the traditional agrarian economy is largely intact and where scant use is made of modern technology in either industry or agriculture. This area, encompassing over a billion people, includes all of non-Soviet Asia except Japan, the South Sea islands, all of Africa north of the Union of South Africa, and virtually all of Latin America except Argentina.

Throughout most of these regions the tempo of population growth is mounting rapidly because death rates are falling while the birth rates remain at very high levels. On the average, the population may be growing by as much as 2 per cent per year, which, if continued, would double the present size of population in thirty-five years. In Mexico and several other Latin American countries, in the Philippines, Taiwan (Formosa) and possibly Egypt, the population is growing at the rate of more than 3 per cent per year, which means that it would be double its present size in twenty-three years.

Population and Economic Growth

Populations that grow rapidly must also expand their economic production rapidly. When populations grow at the rate of 2 or 3 per cent per year, only that part of the country's expanded economic production which runs above 2 or 3 per cent can be used for the improvement of living conditions. Such gains are difficult to obtain. True, in the United States during the past century, our economic production probably rose by 3 or 4 per cent per year. However, we had a vast, empty and rich country, much foreign capital and a relatively well-educated population.

The underdeveloped countries, by contrast, are frequently densely settled, often more than seven times as densely settled as we are now. Because available new land is scarce, the expansion of economic production is particularly dependent on technological innovations requiring capital. But foreign capital is scarce, and incomes are so low that savings are small.

No one knows exactly how much new capital is necessary to produce a given expansion of income, but it is safe to assume that populations growing at between 2 and 3 per cent per year must save and invest between 5 and 15 per cent of their annual incomes just to keep even. Any improvement in economic conditions must come from savings above these figures. Our own savings have been substantially higher, but it is easy to accumulate savings in a prosperous economy. The implications are entirely different for the poor economy, whose population frequently spends over 60 per cent of its income on food alone and remains seriously undernourished.

Higher levels of savings can be and have been forced in Russia and possibly in China. Grain has been sold on the world market to purchase industrial materials during a domestic famine. But such action does not represent an acceptable solution to the problem. There are many brutal ways of checking population growth, but we must find those that are acceptable in humanitarian terms, those that we would advocate if our own lives and those of our children were involved.

There is a further difficulty connected with population growth. Because of their very high birth rates, the populations of the underdeveloped countries are heavily concentrated in the ages below the working years of life. Most underdeveloped countries have more than 40 per cent of their total population under the age of fifteen. By contrast, the developed countries seldom have as much as 30 per cent in that group. This burden of youth dependency is a heavy one. But in spite of the small proportions in the working ages, there is a great deal of under-employment. This ineffective use of the labor force only documents the economic difficulty inherent in the shortage of land and capital. Such shortages are, as we have seen, greatly intensified by population growth.

The conclusion is inescapable that rapid population growth lifts the rate of economic growth required to improve living conditions and at the same time, by expanding consumer needs, restricts the accumulation of capital that is essential for the technological innovations needed to attain such economic growth.

Factors in Population Expansion

The cause of the rapidly mounting rates of population growth is clear. It is the spectacular reduction of the death rate made possible by the medical discoveries of the past three decades. The use of sulfa drugs, antibiotics and insecticides such as DDT has permitted the control of infectious diseases on a scale and with a speed hitherto impossible. Death rates in many of the underdeveloped countries are declining three to five times as fast as they did in nineteenth-century Europe. Ceylon, for example, cut its death rate in half in ten years. Ceylon, Taiwan, Singapore and a number of Latin American countries have death rates that are much the same as those of the modernized West—approximately ten per 1,000 population per year. The low rates come partly from rapidly mounting life expectancies. But they come also from the rapid growth yielded by high birth rates, which tends to concentrate the populations in the young ages where the risks of death are rather low.

In most of the regions with which we are dealing, death rates are much higher than ten. Even so, progress has been made. No one knows the exact pre-war death rates of India and China but they were probably a little above thirty during the good years and much higher during years of major epidemics. Now they are probably in the low twenties. Moreover, there is no reason why they should not continue to fall rapidly in response to the expanding public health programs of both countries. In still other areas, notably those of Central Africa, less progress has been made, but there too, death rates will drop as soon as modern public health programs can be introduced.

It is important to note that this control of disease has been achieved by methods that depend little on the cooperation of individual members of the population. Crews spray homes and vaccinate and inoculate assembled villages. Even treatment of the individual by sulfa drugs and antibiotics is brief, convenient and inexpensive. In short, populations that in any case are rather willing to cooperate with efforts to improve their health have little cooperating to do. Health is almost brought to them. The new methods of controlling disease have another result. We have now learned how to keep death rates amazingly low even under conditions of appalling poverty.

Meanwhile, nearly all underdeveloped countries have more than forty births a year for each 1,000 population. A few report lower figures but in such cases the registration of births can be shown to be incomplete. Birth rates above forty-five are not at all unusual, particularly in Latin America and the Middle East. With modern death rates, the implication of such birth rates for growth is clear.

Fallacies in Current Thinking

Against this background, let us review briefly some of the misunderstandings that are prevalent here and abroad.

One is that if the birth rates are reduced, populations will decline. But if efforts in the field of public health are at all adequate, the birth rates of the underdeveloped areas could fall to less than half of their present level and there would still be moderately rapid population growth. In the absence of barbarities such as compulsory mass sterilization, as much as a 50 per cent reduction of the birth rate seems outside the bounds of possibility in the foreseeable future. Given public order, the maximum reasonable objective is that of reducing birth rates sufficiently to hold the growth of population well below the expansion of the economy.

Extremists occasionally say that the West is interested in reducing the birth rates of underdeveloped countries as a substitute for economic development. The view is well publicized by Communist propaganda. Nothing could be further from the truth. Increased production must underlie any solution to the problems of poverty. The real danger is that they cannot be solved even with economic development unless there is some check on population growth. The hope of those seeking to reduce birth rates is not to find a substitute for economic development but a means of increasing the speed with which economic development can provide better living conditions for the population. The danger is that it will only provide more people living in much the same state of poverty.

We have every reason to suppose that it is virtually impossible to change the reproductive behavior of the traditional peasant society by a further intensification of its poverty. In a time when popular aspirations for health and prosperity are rising throughout the world, policies of repression are much more likely to bring revolution, disorganization and mounting death rates than to stimulate the spread of the small-family ideal.

There is also the completely opposite view which holds that only economic development is required. The advocates of this position point to the fact that birth rates have fallen in the context of urban-industrial development and popular education in the Western world. We should, they say, forget about population growth entirely and concentrate on urban-industrial development, public education, health and improving the status of women.

This view receives support from some individuals who are opposed to various methods of birth control on moral grounds and seem to think they can escape from the difficulty of accepting contraception by advocating urban-industrial development. But there is compelling evidence that whenever the forces of modernization have developed the incentive for birth restriction, the restriction itself has been accomplished mainly by the spread of contraceptive practice. Notwithstanding claims to the contrary, reductions in the birth rate have been achieved overwhelmingly through voluntary means, by not marrying, or by preventing conception or by interfering with the survival of the fetus. People opposed to birth control would be in a more tenable position if they opposed economic development and education on the grounds that such innovations are likely to stimulate the spread of contraception.

The thesis that birth rates will decline in the presence of economic development says nothing about the speed with which a downward trend of fertility may be expected to get underway or about the number of times the population would double before birth rates and death rates came into fairly close balance. In Japan, where there has been rapid modernization since the 1860s, the population has increased threefold and the rate of growth is still substantial—in spite of the fact that it now has the lowest fertility in the world. The multiplication encountered during the transition from high to low birth and death rates was even larger in the West. There are grounds for doubting that the automatic processes of social change will bring a sufficiently rapid adjustment. Today the fertility of married women is much the same in the major cities of India as in the rural villages, and the same lack of contrast probably prevails in many other countries.

Problems in Contraception

Finally, there is the group, to which the writer belongs, that is convinced of the importance of taking energetic measures to spread the practice of birth control. The group is large and is growing very rapidly in several of the underdeveloped countries. This was amply demonstrated in New Delhi at the International Conference on Planned Parenthood, which was opened by Prime Minister Nehru and in which participated many leaders of academic, medical and public life—drawn from a wide variety of underdeveloped countries as well as from the West.

There is mounting interest in stimulating the decline of

the birth rate by spreading contraceptive practice, but in view of the dimensions of the problem only the smallest start has been made. There are grave difficulties and wide divergencies of opinion as to the proper course to take. Much of the disagreement comes from the fact that no effort to promote restrictive practices in the peasant villages has yet proved very successful. Too few attempts have been made to test inexpensive but sophisticated programs.

Admittedly, it is difficult to use existing contraceptive methods under the conditions of the usual peasant home—which lacks privacy, sanitary facilities and suitable storage places. Neither is the situation favorable for the practice of periodic abstinence. Frequent confinements and a heavy incidence of infection, anemia and malnutrition interfere with the establishment of predictably regular menstrual cycles.

Moreover, the level of education is so low that many women find it impossible to keep track of their calendars. Ingenuity has been used to assist them. In one experiment, a string of green and red glass beads was supplied to each woman with instructions that she should move one bead along each day, abstaining on the "red days." A few were used appropriately but in more cases there were accidental mix-ups or the beads served either as jewelry or as playthings for the baby. One patient is reported to have said that the beads were very good but that her husband steadfastly refused to eat them!

Such difficulties have led some people to conclude that success is impossible until we have developed a contraceptive method that is effective, convenient, cheap and safe even under conditions of gross misuse. It is this need that has stimulated the interest in research for a contraceptive tablet to be taken by mouth.

Unquestionably, there is great need for research to find better methods of fertility control and to enhance all aspects of our knowledge of human reproduction. Until recently, pathetically little was being done. Now hopes are high that within something like five years we shall have several greatly improved methods.

Many people seem to think that the problem would be solved as soon as we could match, on the side of fertility, the scientific advances with which we control mortality. Unfortunately, this conclusion overlooks the fundamental differences between mortality and fertility. No one wants to die. But many people want large families. To still more, the idea of not accepting happily the number of children that "God sends" has never occurred and, when proposed, is likely to be abhorrent. Throughout the ages of inevitably high mortality, the selective processes of survival have placed a high value on those societies that inculcated the desire for many births. The rewards and penalties of family and community life in matters of security and prestige are heavily oriented in favor of the parents of many children, particularly of many sons. These ideas have been deeply imbedded for centuries in the most fundamental institutions and beliefs and are difficult to change.

Technological efficiency in fertility control will be an invaluable assistance to couples who are hesitant, frightened and weakly motivated toward restricting the number of their births. But new and efficient methods will have their major impact only as the older ideals concerning appropriate reproduction are replaced by a widespread and deeply felt awareness of the advantages of fewer births. In sharp contrast to the problem of reducing deaths, the basic problem in the control of fertility is that of moving men's minds. In free societies, the choices governing procreation must ultimately remain those of individual couples.

The Need for Understanding

There is a wide range of positive action open to us. In the first place, we need to foster among the articulate and politically active elements of the regions concerned a better understanding of the relations of population growth to health, education and prosperity. Often, as in India, Pakistan, Egypt and Ceylon, this understanding is already present at the highest levels of government. But a more broadly based understanding is needed to provide political support for programs of the required scope. In all too many areas there is little interest or understanding, even at the highest levels.

It is unlikely that we in the West can do much to promote this understanding directly. Our opinions are viewed with too much suspicion to have a maximum effect. One of the most useful things we can do is to train students from under-developed areas to study their own problems by modern scientific methods. The findings of their own specialists, lucidly interpreted to the public, will carry much more weight than anything we can say.

In this field of scientific training, a good beginning has been made by the United Nations, governmental exchange programs and the work of private foundations. Two regional centers for demographic training and research have been started under the auspices of the United Nations, one in India and one in Chile. In addition, fellowship programs are bringing students to the West for training. At Princeton, for example, students have come for advanced training in population research from eighteen different countries. These students have already done much to broaden the understanding of the issues in their own countries. The research of the United Nations has also been valuable in helping governments to determine the facts for themselves.

Widespread knowledge of population problems only helps gain public support for needed action. Changes in individual behavior come for private reasons—such as the realization by married couples that, under modern conditions of health, their family life will be enriched if there are fewer births. We must learn how to impart this understanding efficiently, but the work itself is so peculiarly sensitive that it had better be undertaken by indigenous agencies. At least at the present stage, our role might well be limited to supplying requested assistance in technical training, consultation and experimental work. These tasks are far from small, and the needed work is scarcely begun.

Bibliography

Brown, H. *The Challenge of Man's Future.* New York: Viking Press, 1954.

Coale, A. J., and Hoover, E. M. *Population Growth and Economic Development in Low-Income Countries.* Princeton: Princeton University Press, 1958.

Fagley, R. M. *The Population Explosion and Christian Responsibility.* New York: Oxford University Press, 1960.

Guttmacher, A. F. "Pills for Population Control?" *Saturday Review,* 1960, 63:6, 50-51.

Hauser, P. M., and Duncan, O. D. (eds.). *The Study of Population: An Inventory and Appraisal.* Chicago: University of Chicago Press, 1959.

Osborn, F. *Population: An International Dilemma*. New York: Population Council, 1958.

Sax, K. *Standing Room Only*. Rev. ed. Boston: Beacon Press, 1960.

Spengler, J. J., and Duncan, O. D. (eds.). *Population Theory and Policy*. Glencoe, Ill.: Free Press, 1956.

Sulloway, A. W. *Birth Control and Catholic Doctrine*. Boston: Beacon Press, 1959.

Part VI Epilogue

14   Man's Role in Nature

JULIAN HUXLEY

Science provides increased control over the forces of nature and so gives us the means of realizing our aims in practice. But it also provides fuller understanding and a truer vision of natural reality. This is in the long run the more important, for our vision of reality helps to determine our aims.

By discovering how to control intra-atomic energy, science has launched us into the Atomic Era, with all its attendant hopes and fears. But by giving us fuller comprehension of nature as a whole, it has set us on the threshold of a greater and more revolutionary age, which I will call the Humanist Era. It is the era in which the evolutionary process, in the person of man, is becoming purposeful and conscious of itself.

Today, for the first time in man's long and strange history, science is revealing a comprehensive picture of the natural universe and of man's place and role in it—in a word, of his destiny.

Thanks to the patient labors of thousands of scientists— biologists and astronomers, geologists and anthropologists, historians and physicists—the universe of nature in which man lives is now revealed as a single process of evolution, vast in its scales of space and time. Man is part of this universal evolving world-stuff. He is made of the same matter, operated by the same energy, as all the stars in all the galaxies.

Most of the universe is lifeless and its portentously slow evolution has produced only simple patterns of organization and little variety. But on our earth (and doubtless on other planetary specks) conditions permitted the appearance of the self-reproducing and self-varying type of matter we call life. With this, natural selection could begin to act and the biological phase of evolution was initiated.

Through natural selection, change—though still slow by human standards—could become much more rapid, and surprising new possibilities could be realized by the world-stuff. From the uniformity and relative simplicity of submicrosopic particles, there was generated the astonishingly rich variety of life, from sea-anemones and ants to cuttlefish and lions, from bacteria and toadstools to daisies and giant trees; the astonishingly high organization of a beehive or a bird; and most astonishing of all, the emergence of mind—living matter's increasing awareness of itself and its surroundings.

Psychosocial Evolution

But there are restrictions on what the blind forces of natural selection can accomplish. A few million years ago, it now appears, living matter had reached the limits of purely material and physiological achievement; only the possibilities of mind remained largely unrealized.

By exploiting the possibilities of mental advance, man became the latest dominant type of life and initiated a new phase of evolution—the human or *psychosocial* phase—which operates much faster than biological evolution and produces new kinds of results. Man's capacity for reason and imagination, coupled with his ability to communicate his ideas by means of the verbal symbols of language, provided him with a new mechanism for evolution, in the shape of cumulative tradition. Pre-human life depended only on the transmission of material particles, the genes in the chromosomes, from one generation to the next. But man can also transmit experience and its results. With this, mind as well as matter acquired the capacity for self-reproduction. Natural selection became subordinate to psychosocial selection, and the human phase of evolution could begin.

Science has also shown man his position in evolutionary time. Life has been evolving on the earth for over two thousand million years. Man-like creatures have existed for only about one million years, and human civilization—with all its achievements—for a bare five thousand. But evolving man can reasonably expect an immensity of future time—another two thousand million or more.

The psychosocial phase of evolution is thus in its infancy; man as the dominant evolutionary type is absurdly young. To adapt a simile of Sir James Jeans: If you represent the biological past by the height of St. Paul's cathedral, then the time since the beginning of agriculture and settled life equals one postage stamp flat on its top. And, unless man destroys himself by nuclear war or other follies, he can look forward to evolving through at least the time-equivalent of another St. Paul's.

Man's place and role in nature is now clear. No other animal can now hope to challenge his dominant position. Only man is capable of further real advance, of major new evolutionary achievement. He and he alone is now responsible for the future of this planet and its inhabitants. In him evolution is at last becoming conscious of itself; his mind is the agency by which evolution can reach new levels of achievement. Man's destiny, we now perceive, is to be the agent of evolution on this earth, realizing richer and ampler possibilities for the evolutionary process and providing greater fulfillment for more human beings.

The revelation of fulfillment as man's most ultimate and comprehensive aim provides us with a criterion for assessing our own psychosocial evolution. Already in its brief course psychosocial evolution has produced real progress—increased expectation of life, less disease, more knowledge, better communications, increase of mechanical power and decrease of physical drudgery, more varied interest and enrichment through creative achievement—in buildings and works of art, in music and spectacle, in discovery and ideas. But it has also produced poverty and crime and slavery and organized cruelty, and its course has been accompanied by constant exploitation, indignity, and slaughter.

In this new perspective, we see that what Père Teilhard de Chardin called the process of hominization—the better realization of man's intrinsic possibilities—has barely begun. Few human beings realize more than a tiny fraction of their capacities, or enjoy any but the most meager degree of possible satisfaction and self-fulfillment. The majority are still illiterate, undernourished and short-lived, and their existence is full of misery and indignity. Nor have human societies realized more than a fraction of their capacities. They provide inadequate opportunities for expression and enjoyment, they still produce more ugliness than beauty, more frustration than fulfillment;

they can easily lead to the dehumanization of life instead of its enrichment.

Psychosocial Science

What has all this to do with science? I would say a great deal. First let us remember that most of what we can properly call advance in psychosocial evolution has stemmed from new or better organized knowledge—whether in the form of traditional skills, sudden inventions, new scientific discoveries, technological improvements or new insights into old problems.

Science is a particularly efficient method for obtaining, organizing and applying knowledge. Though modern science is barely three centuries old, it has led to the most unexpected discoveries and the most spectacular practical results. Scientific method involves controlled observation of fact, rational interpretation by way of hypothesis, the publication and discussion of procedures and results and the further checking of hypothesis against fact. The use of scientific method has proved to be the best way of obtaining fuller intellectual understanding and increased practical control, in all fields where it has been tried. It leads inevitably toward more and fuller truth, to an increasing body of more firmly established factual knowledge, and more coherent principles and ideas.

Science is often used to denote only the natural sciences; but this is a false restriction, which springs from the historical fact that scientific method could be more readily applied to simpler subjects and so first became effectively applied in non-human fields. But it can be applied to all natural phenomena, however complex, provided that we take account of their special peculiarities and go to the trouble of devising appropriate methods for dealing with them.

Today, the time has come to apply scientific method to man and all his works. We have made a piecemeal beginning —with psychology, economics, anthropology, linguistics, sociology and so forth. But we need a comprehensive approach to the human field as a whole. We already have physical science, chemical science and biological science; to deal with man as a natural phenomenon, we must develop *psychosocial* science.

The primary job of psychosocial science will be to describe and analyze the course and mechanism of psychosocial evolution in scientific terms. It will also include a science of human possibilities. What are the possibilities of man and his nature, individually and collectively? How is their realization helped or hindered by different types of psychosocial environment? How can we estimate human fulfillment; in what ways and to what extent can it be promoted by changes in psychosocial organization? In particular, such a science will involve a radical re-thinking of man's systems of education—their aims, content and techniques.

The value of such an approach and such criteria is clear when we look at concrete problems. Two new challenges have recently appeared on the evolutionary scene—the threat of over-population and the promise of excess leisure. The population problem obstinately resists solution in terms of power politics, economics or religion, but the criterion of greater fulfillment immediately lights it up and indicates the general lines of the policy we should pursue in reconciling quantity with quality of human life.

The new possibilities opened up by science are exerting two effects on psychosocial evolution. Increased scientific control over the forces of nature has produced a flood of new conveniences and comforts, and has led directly to death control and the recent alarming increase of human numbers. But the knowledge that healthier and longer life is possible, and that technology can provide higher standards of living and enjoyment, has changed the attitude of the vast under-privileged majority; they are demanding that the new possibilities shall be more abundantly realized.

The next step must be to grasp the fact that the quantitative possibilities are not unlimited. Unless present-day man controls the exploitation of natural resources, he will impoverish his descendants; unless he supplements death control with birth control, he will become the cancer of the planet—ruining his earthly habitation and himself with it.

The leisure problem is equally fundamental. Having to decide what we shall do with our leisure is inevitably forcing us to re-examine the purpose of human existence, and to ask what fulfillment really means. This, I repeat, involves a comprehensive survey of human possibilities and the methods of realizing them; it also implies a survey of the obstacles to their realization.

The Process of Fulfillment

Let us summarize the new picture of human destiny from a slightly different angle.

Man is the latest dominant type of life, but he is also a very imperfect kind of being. He is equipped with a modicum of intelligence, but also with an array of conflicting passions and desires. He can be reasonable but is often extremely stupid. He has impulses to sympathy and love, but also to cruelty and hatred. He is capable of moral action but also has inevitable capacities for sin and error.

As a result, the course of psychosocial evolution has been erratic, wasteful and full of imperfection. It is easy to take a pessimistic view of man's history in general, and of his present situation in particular, where force and fear have become magnified on a gigantic scale.

But when we survey the process as a whole, it looks more hopeful. During its course, there has been progress. Progress has always been the result of the discovery, dissemination or application of human knowledge, and human knowledge has shown a cumulative increase. Furthermore, the erratic course of past psychosocial evolution was largely due to man as a species being divided against himself, and not having discovered any single overriding aim.

There is now a dramatic change in process. The human world has become inextricably interlocked with itself; the separate parts of the psychosocial process are being forced to converge toward some sort of organized unity. We are at last able and indeed compelled to think in terms of a single aim for mankind, while our increasing knowledge is enabling us to define our aim in relation to reality instead of in terms of wish-fulfillment. Our knowledge of our imperfections and limitations is helping to define the possibilities of our improvement.

This marks a critical point in history. We have discovered psychosocial evolution as a complex but natural phenomenon, to be explored and controlled like other natural phenomena. Up till now, it has operated in erratic and often undesirable fashion, with self-contradictory aims. We now see that it could be transformed into an orderly mechanism for securing desirable results.

The idea of greater fulfillment for all mankind could become a powerful motive force, capable of influencing the direction of future evolution, and of overriding the more obvious motives of immediate personal or national self-interest. But it can only do so if it and its implications are properly understood, and made comprehensible to the bulk of men, all over the world. For this we need not only an extension of science but a reorientation of education; not only more knowledge, but also a better expression and a wider dissemination of ideas.

We must not imagine that the fuller realization of possibilities will be accomplished without effort, conflict or suffering. This is inherent in the nature of man and of the psychosocial process—but so is hope.

The individual human brain and mind is the most complicated and highly organized piece of machinery that has ever existed on this earth. So-called electronic brains can perform extraordinary tasks with superhuman rapidity, but they have to be given their instructions by men. The human organism can give instructions to itself, and can perform tasks outside the range of any inanimate machine. Though at the outset it is a feeble instrument equipped with conflicting tendencies, it can in the course of its development achieve a high degree of integration and performance.

It is up to us to make the best use of this marvelous piece of living machinery. Instead of taking it for granted, or ignorantly abusing it, we must cherish it, try to understand its development and explore its capacities.

The collective human organism, embodied in the psychosocial process, is an equally extraordinary piece of machinery. It is the mechanism for realizing human destiny. It can discover new aims for itself and devise new methods for realizing them, but it is still primitive and inefficient. It is up to us to improve it, as we have improved our inanimate machines. Our ignorance about its potentialities is profound; therefore our immediate task is to understand the first principles of its operation, and think out their consequences.

A Rational Optimism

Thus the new vision we owe to science is one of real though tempered optimism. It gives us a measure of significance and rational hope in a world which appeared irrational and meaningless. It shows us man's place and role in the universe. He is the earth's reservoir of evolutionary possibility— the servant of evolution but at the same time its youthful master. His destiny is to pursue greater fulfillment through a better ordering of the psychosocial process. That is his extraordinary privilege, and also his supreme duty.

Our new vision assures us that human life could gradually be transformed from a competitive struggle against blind fate into a great collective enterprise, consciously undertaken. We see that enterprise as one for greater fulfillment through the better realization of human possibilities.

It is for us to accept this new revelation given us by science, to examine it and explore all its implications—secure in the knowledge that ideas help to determine events, that more understanding leads to more appropriate action, that

scientific truth is an indispensable weapon against stupidity
and wickedness and the other enemies of fulfillment and that
true vision is the parent of progress.

Bibliography

Dobzhansky, T. *The Biological Basis of Human Freedom.* New
York: Columbia University Press, 1956.

Huxley, J. *Man in the Modern World.* New York: New American Library, 1948.

———. *Religion without Revelation.* Rev. ed. New York: New
American Library, 1957.

———. *New Bottles for New Wine.* New York: Harper, 1957.

———. "Man's Challenge: The Use of the Earth." *Horizon,* 1958,
1:1, 48-55.

Morain, L. and M. *Humanism As the Next Step.* Boston: Beacon
Press, 1954.

Muller, H. J. "Science for Humanity." *Bulletin of the Atomic
Scientists,* 1959, 15, 146-150, 176.

Riddle, O. *The Unleashing of Evolutionary Thought.* New York:
Vantage Press, 1954.

Simpson, G. G. *The Meaning of Evolution.* Rev. ed. New York:
New American Library, 1951.

———. "Darwin Led Us into This Modern World." *Humanist,*
1959, 19, 267-275.

Contributors

ERNEST E. BAYLES is professor of education at the University of Kansas.

HADLEY CANTRIL is chairman of the Institute for International Social Research at Princeton University.

BROCK CHISHOLM is a Canadian psychiatrist, formerly director of the World Health Organization.

RUDOLF DREIKURS is professor of psychiatry at the Chicago Medical School and director of the Alfred Adler Institute.

LAWRENCE K. FRANK is retired and resides in Belmont, Massachusetts. Formerly he was director of the Caroline Zachry Institute of Human Development in New York City.

ERICH FROMM lectures in psychology and psychiatry at the National University of Mexico and is a Fellow at the William Alanson White Institute in New York City.

JULIAN HUXLEY is a British biologist, formerly director of the United Nations Educational, Scientific and Cultural Organization.

SAMUEL JACOBS was Washington representative of the United Auto Workers Union from 1951 until his death in 1959.

Y. H. KRIKORIAN is professor of philosophy at the City College of New York.

ALFRED E. KUENZLI is associate professor of psychology at Southern Illinois University.

FRANK W. NOTESTEIN is president of the Population Council and past director of the Office of Population Research at Princeton University.

CARL R. ROGERS is professor of psychology and psychiatry at the University of Wisconsin.

THEODORE W. SCHULTZ is professor of economics at the University of Chicago and chairman of the Research Advisory Board of the Committee for Economic Development.

DONALD SNYGG is chairman of the psychology department at the Oswego campus of the State University of New York.

Acknowledgments

The materials included in this volume have, for the most part, appeared in other places within recent years. All of the papers have been revised or modified in some way to suit the present style and purpose. We have hoped to achieve a maximum of meaning and communication while, at the same time, recognizing the need for economy and brevity.

In several instances, the contributors have added paragraphs so as to express their most recent views. In other cases, they have agreed to omit material that was dated or not very relevant to the main theme of the symposium.

The editor wishes to express his appreciation to the authors and publishers who granted permission to reprint these selections. The original sources are as follows:

BAYLES, E. E. "A Relativistic Religion." *Phi Delta Kappan,* 1958, 40, 33-36.

CANTRIL, H. "The Nature of Faith." *Journal of Individual Psychology,* 1957, 13, 24-37.

CHISHOLM, B. *Prescription for Survival.* New York: Columbia University Press, 1957. Pp. 26-48.

DREIKURS, R. "The Religion of Democracy." *Humanist,* 1955, 15, 210-215, 266-273.

FRANK, L. K. "Freedom for the Personality." *Psychiatry,* 1940, 3, 341-349.

FROMM, E. "Faith As a Character Trait." *Psychiatry,* 1942, 5, 307-319.

HUXLEY, J. "The Future of Man." *Bulletin of the Atomic Scientists,*
   1959, 15, 402-404, 409.

JACOBS, S. "The Richer Rich and Poorer Poor." *Humanist,* 1959,
   19, 215-224.

KRIKORIAN, Y. H. "The Ethics of Naturalism." *New Republic,* 1949,
   121:16, 32-36.

KUENZLI, A. E. "An Objective Basis for Ethics." *Humanist,* 1960,
   20, 154-160.

NOTESTEIN, F. W. "Poverty and Population." *Atlantic Monthly,*
   1959, 204:5, 84-87.

ROGERS, C. R. "A Therapist's View of the Good Life." *Humanist,*
   1957, 17, 291-300.

SCHULTZ, T. W. "Human Wealth and Economic Growth." *Humanist,* 1959, 19, 71-81.

SNYGG, D. "The Psychological Basis of Human Values." In A. D.
   Ward (ed.), *Goals of Economic Life.* New York: Harper, 1953.
   Pp. 335-364.

The Humanist, in the foregoing references, is published
by the American Humanist Association in Yellow Springs,
Ohio, and is to be distinguished from a British periodical bear-
ing the same name.

   Permission to reprint the article by Samuel Jacobs was
granted by Max M. Kampelman, executor of the estate.